50 Easy-Peasy Sheet Pan Supper Recipes for Home

By: Kelly Johnson

Table of Contents

- Sheet Pan Lemon Garlic Herb Chicken with Vegetables
- Honey Balsamic Glazed Salmon with Asparagus
- Teriyaki Chicken with Broccoli and Bell Peppers
- Garlic Parmesan Roasted Shrimp and Broccoli
- Lemon Dill Sheet Pan Cod with Roasted Vegetables
- Mediterranean Chicken with Olives and Cherry Tomatoes
- Pesto Parmesan Crusted Chicken with Brussels Sprouts
- BBQ Ranch Chicken Drumsticks with Sweet Potato Wedges
- Sheet Pan Fajitas with Steak and Bell Peppers
- Harissa Roasted Vegetables with Spiced Chicken Thighs
- Maple Dijon Glazed Pork Chops with Brussels Sprouts
- Cajun Shrimp and Sausage with Okra
- Greek Lemon Chicken with Potatoes and Green Beans
- Italian Sausage with Peppers, Onions, and Potatoes
- Orange Glazed Salmon with Asparagus and Broccolini
- Sheet Pan Teriyaki Beef and Broccoli
- Lemon Herb Butter Baked Cod with Zucchini
- Herb Crusted Pork Tenderloin with Carrots and Potatoes
- Mediterranean Veggie Bake with Chickpeas
- Maple Mustard Glazed Chicken Thighs with Brussels Sprouts
- Sheet Pan Garlic Butter Shrimp with Asparagus
- Teriyaki Salmon with Snap Peas and Red Onion
- Herb Roasted Turkey Breast with Fall Vegetables
- Honey Garlic Chicken Thighs with Brussels Sprouts
- Lemon Butter Baked Tilapia with Roasted Vegetables
- Sheet Pan Pesto Chicken with Cherry Tomatoes and Mozzarella
- Chipotle Lime Chicken with Corn and Black Beans
- Teriyaki Tofu and Broccoli for a vegetarian option
- Lemon Rosemary Roasted Cornish Hens with Root Vegetables
- Sheet Pan Caprese Chicken with Balsamic Glaze
- Spicy Maple Glazed Salmon with Sweet Potato Wedges
- Herb Roasted Chicken Drumsticks with Cauliflower
- Lemon Garlic Butter Shrimp with Asparagus
- Baked Greek Chicken with Artichokes and Kalamata Olives
- Cajun Roasted Sausage and Vegetables

- Mediterranean Baked Cod with Feta and Tomatoes
- Pesto Ranch Chicken Thighs with Brussels Sprouts
- Sesame Ginger Glazed Salmon with Broccoli
- BBQ Ranch Chicken and Potatoes
- Spicy Maple Glazed Chicken Drumsticks with Brussels Sprouts
- Lemon Herb Sheet Pan Pork Chops with Green Beans
- Mediterranean Chickpea and Eggplant Bake
- Orange Glazed Chicken Thighs with Carrots and Broccoli
- Sheet Pan Shrimp Scampi with Asparagus
- Hoisin Glazed Sheet Pan Pork with Cabbage
- Lemon Garlic Butter Baked Cod with Roasted Vegetables
- Honey Mustard Glazed Chicken with Brussels Sprouts
- Teriyaki Tempeh with Mixed Vegetables for a vegetarian option
- Sheet Pan Italian Sausage and Peppers
- Baked Lemon Butter Shrimp with Zucchini and Cherry Tomatoes

Sheet Pan Lemon Garlic Herb Chicken with Vegetables

Ingredients:

For the Chicken:

- 4 boneless, skinless chicken breasts
- 3 tablespoons olive oil
- 4 cloves garlic, minced
- Zest and juice of 1 lemon
- 1 teaspoon dried thyme
- 1 teaspoon dried rosemary
- 1 teaspoon dried oregano
- Salt and pepper to taste

For the Vegetables:

- 1 pound baby potatoes, halved
- 1 pound baby carrots
- 1 red bell pepper, sliced
- 1 yellow bell pepper, sliced
- 1 zucchini, sliced
- 1 cup cherry tomatoes
- 2 tablespoons olive oil
- Salt and pepper to taste

Instructions:

Preheat Oven:
- Preheat your oven to 400°F (200°C).

Prepare Chicken Marinade:
- In a bowl, mix together olive oil, minced garlic, lemon zest, lemon juice, dried thyme, dried rosemary, dried oregano, salt, and pepper.

Marinate Chicken:
- Place the chicken breasts in a resealable plastic bag or a shallow dish. Pour half of the marinade over the chicken, ensuring each piece is well coated. Let it marinate while you prepare the vegetables.

Prepare Vegetables:

- In a large mixing bowl, combine baby potatoes, baby carrots, sliced bell peppers, sliced zucchini, cherry tomatoes, olive oil, salt, and pepper. Toss until the vegetables are evenly coated.

Assemble on Sheet Pan:
- Line a large sheet pan with parchment paper or lightly grease it. Place the marinated chicken breasts on one side and arrange the vegetables on the other side.

Drizzle Remaining Marinade:
- Drizzle the remaining marinade over the vegetables and chicken.

Bake:
- Bake in the preheated oven for 25-30 minutes or until the chicken is cooked through and the vegetables are tender, tossing the vegetables halfway through for even cooking.

Serve:
- Once cooked, remove from the oven, let it rest for a few minutes, and then serve the Sheet Pan Lemon Garlic Herb Chicken with Vegetables.

Enjoy this delicious and wholesome meal with the aromatic blend of lemon and herbs.

The convenience of a sheet pan dinner makes cleanup a breeze, and the flavors are sure to be a hit!

Honey Balsamic Glazed Salmon with Asparagus

Ingredients:

For the Salmon:

- 4 salmon fillets
- 3 tablespoons balsamic vinegar
- 2 tablespoons honey (or a keto-friendly sweetener for a low-carb version)
- 2 tablespoons soy sauce (or tamari for a gluten-free option)
- 2 cloves garlic, minced
- 1 teaspoon Dijon mustard
- Salt and pepper to taste
- Fresh parsley, chopped (for garnish)

For the Asparagus:

- 1 bunch of asparagus, woody ends trimmed
- 1 tablespoon olive oil
- Salt and pepper to taste

Instructions:

Preheat Oven:
- Preheat your oven to 400°F (200°C).

Prepare Glaze:
- In a small bowl, whisk together balsamic vinegar, honey, soy sauce, minced garlic, Dijon mustard, salt, and pepper. This is your glaze for the salmon.

Prepare Salmon:
- Place the salmon fillets on a parchment-lined or lightly greased baking sheet.

Brush Salmon with Glaze:
- Brush the salmon fillets generously with the honey balsamic glaze, ensuring they are well coated on all sides.

Prepare Asparagus:
- In a separate bowl, toss the trimmed asparagus with olive oil, salt, and pepper.

Assemble on Sheet Pan:

- Arrange the glazed salmon fillets on one side of the baking sheet and the seasoned asparagus on the other side.

Bake:
- Bake in the preheated oven for 12-15 minutes or until the salmon is cooked through and flakes easily with a fork. The asparagus should be tender but still crisp.

Broil (Optional):
- For a caramelized finish, you can broil the salmon and asparagus for an additional 2-3 minutes, keeping a close eye to prevent burning.

Garnish and Serve:
- Remove from the oven, garnish with chopped fresh parsley, and serve the Honey Balsamic Glazed Salmon with Asparagus.

This sheet pan dinner offers a perfect balance of sweet and savory flavors. It's a quick and elegant option for a delicious weeknight meal. Enjoy!

Teriyaki Chicken with Broccoli and Bell Peppers

Ingredients:

For the Teriyaki Sauce:

- 1/4 cup soy sauce (or tamari for a gluten-free option)
- 2 tablespoons honey or a keto-friendly sweetener
- 1 tablespoon rice vinegar
- 1 tablespoon sesame oil
- 1 clove garlic, minced
- 1 teaspoon grated ginger

For the Chicken and Vegetables:

- 4 boneless, skinless chicken breasts, cut into bite-sized pieces
- 2 cups broccoli florets
- 1 red bell pepper, sliced
- 1 yellow bell pepper, sliced
- 1 tablespoon olive oil
- Salt and pepper to taste
- Sesame seeds and chopped green onions for garnish (optional)

Instructions:

Preheat Oven:
- Preheat your oven to 400°F (200°C).

Make Teriyaki Sauce:
- In a small bowl, whisk together soy sauce, honey, rice vinegar, sesame oil, minced garlic, and grated ginger to create the teriyaki sauce.

Prepare Chicken and Vegetables:
- Place the chicken pieces, broccoli florets, and sliced bell peppers on a sheet pan.

Drizzle with Olive Oil:
- Drizzle the olive oil over the chicken and vegetables. Season with salt and pepper to taste.

Toss with Teriyaki Sauce:
- Pour about half of the teriyaki sauce over the chicken and vegetables. Toss everything to coat evenly.

Bake:
- Bake in the preheated oven for 20-25 minutes or until the chicken is cooked through, and the vegetables are tender, stirring halfway through.

Drizzle with More Sauce:
- Drizzle the remaining teriyaki sauce over the cooked chicken and vegetables before serving.

Garnish and Serve:
- Optionally, garnish with sesame seeds and chopped green onions for added flavor and presentation.

Enjoy this Teriyaki Chicken with Broccoli and Bell Peppers over rice, cauliflower rice, or on its own. The sweet and savory teriyaki glaze adds a delicious Asian-inspired touch to this easy and wholesome sheet pan meal.

Garlic Parmesan Roasted Shrimp and Broccoli

Ingredients:

- 1 pound large shrimp, peeled and deveined
- 4 cups broccoli florets
- 3 tablespoons olive oil
- 4 cloves garlic, minced
- 1/2 cup grated Parmesan cheese
- 1 teaspoon dried oregano
- 1 teaspoon dried basil
- 1/2 teaspoon crushed red pepper flakes (optional, for some heat)
- Salt and black pepper to taste
- Lemon wedges for serving

Instructions:

Preheat Oven:
- Preheat your oven to 400°F (200°C).

Prepare Shrimp and Broccoli:
- In a large mixing bowl, combine the shrimp and broccoli florets.

Make Garlic Parmesan Mixture:
- In a separate bowl, whisk together olive oil, minced garlic, grated Parmesan cheese, dried oregano, dried basil, crushed red pepper flakes (if using), salt, and black pepper.

Coat Shrimp and Broccoli:
- Pour the garlic Parmesan mixture over the shrimp and broccoli. Toss until everything is evenly coated.

Arrange on Sheet Pan:
- Spread the shrimp and broccoli mixture on a baking sheet in a single layer.

Roast in the Oven:
- Roast in the preheated oven for 12-15 minutes or until the shrimp are pink and opaque, and the broccoli is tender-crisp.

Broil for Crispy Top:
- Optionally, broil for an additional 2-3 minutes to get a crispy and golden top on the shrimp and broccoli. Keep an eye on it to prevent burning.

Serve:
- Remove from the oven, squeeze fresh lemon juice over the top, and serve the Garlic Parmesan Roasted Shrimp and Broccoli immediately.

This easy and delicious sheet pan meal is perfect for a quick and healthy dinner. The combination of garlic, Parmesan, and roasted flavors adds a delightful twist to shrimp and broccoli. Enjoy!

Lemon Dill Sheet Pan Cod with Roasted Vegetables

Ingredients:

For the Cod:

- 4 cod fillets (about 6 ounces each)
- 2 tablespoons olive oil
- Zest and juice of 1 lemon
- 2 cloves garlic, minced
- 1 tablespoon fresh dill, chopped
- Salt and black pepper to taste

For the Roasted Vegetables:

- 4 cups mixed vegetables (such as cherry tomatoes, bell peppers, zucchini, and red onion), chopped
- 2 tablespoons olive oil
- Salt and black pepper to taste

Instructions:

Preheat Oven:
- Preheat your oven to 400°F (200°C).

Prepare Cod Marinade:
- In a small bowl, whisk together olive oil, lemon zest, lemon juice, minced garlic, chopped dill, salt, and black pepper to create the marinade for the cod.

Marinate Cod:
- Place the cod fillets in a shallow dish or a resealable plastic bag. Pour the marinade over the cod, ensuring each fillet is well coated. Let it marinate while you prepare the vegetables.

Prepare Vegetables:
- In a separate bowl, toss the chopped mixed vegetables with olive oil, salt, and black pepper.

Arrange on Sheet Pan:
- Line a large sheet pan with parchment paper. Arrange the marinated cod fillets on one side and the seasoned vegetables on the other.

Roast in the Oven:

- Roast in the preheated oven for 15-20 minutes or until the cod is opaque and flakes easily with a fork, and the vegetables are tender.

Broil for Color:
- Optionally, broil for an additional 2-3 minutes to add a golden color to the cod and vegetables. Keep an eye on it to prevent burning.

Serve:
- Remove from the oven and serve the Lemon Dill Sheet Pan Cod with Roasted Vegetables immediately. Garnish with additional fresh dill and lemon wedges if desired.

This sheet pan cod recipe is a light and flavorful option for a quick and healthy dinner. The combination of lemon and dill enhances the natural taste of the cod, and the roasted vegetables add a colorful and nutritious touch to the meal. Enjoy!

Mediterranean Chicken with Olives and Cherry Tomatoes

Ingredients:

For the Chicken:

- 4 boneless, skinless chicken breasts
- 2 tablespoons olive oil
- 3 cloves garlic, minced
- 1 teaspoon dried oregano
- 1 teaspoon dried thyme
- 1 teaspoon dried rosemary
- Salt and black pepper to taste
- Juice of 1 lemon

For the Vegetables:

- 1 cup cherry tomatoes, halved
- 1/2 cup Kalamata olives, pitted
- 1/2 cup green olives, pitted
- 1 red onion, thinly sliced
- 2 tablespoons olive oil
- Salt and black pepper to taste

Optional Garnish:

- Feta cheese, crumbled
- Fresh parsley, chopped

Instructions:

Preheat Oven:
- Preheat your oven to 400°F (200°C).

Prepare Chicken Marinade:
- In a bowl, mix together olive oil, minced garlic, dried oregano, dried thyme, dried rosemary, salt, black pepper, and lemon juice.

Marinate Chicken:

- Place the chicken breasts in a shallow dish or a resealable plastic bag. Pour half of the marinade over the chicken, ensuring each piece is well coated. Let it marinate while you prepare the vegetables.

Prepare Vegetables:
- In a separate bowl, toss the halved cherry tomatoes, Kalamata olives, green olives, and thinly sliced red onion with olive oil, salt, and black pepper.

Arrange on Sheet Pan:
- Line a large sheet pan with parchment paper. Place the marinated chicken breasts on one side and the seasoned vegetables on the other.

Roast in the Oven:
- Roast in the preheated oven for 20-25 minutes or until the chicken is cooked through and the vegetables are tender, tossing the vegetables halfway through for even cooking.

Serve:
- Once cooked, remove from the oven, garnish with crumbled feta cheese and chopped fresh parsley if desired, and serve the Mediterranean Chicken with Olives and Cherry Tomatoes.

This sheet pan meal captures the essence of Mediterranean cuisine with its vibrant colors and robust flavors. The combination of herbs, olives, and juicy cherry tomatoes creates a delightful and wholesome dish. Enjoy!

Pesto Parmesan Crusted Chicken with Brussels Sprouts

Ingredients:

For the Chicken:

- 4 boneless, skinless chicken breasts
- Salt and black pepper, to taste
- 1 cup basil pesto (store-bought or homemade)
- 1 cup grated Parmesan cheese
- 1 cup breadcrumbs (optional, for added crunch)

For the Brussels Sprouts:

- 1 pound Brussels sprouts, trimmed and halved
- 2 tablespoons olive oil
- Salt and black pepper, to taste

Instructions:

Preheat the Oven:

Preheat your oven to 400°F (200°C).
Prepare the Chicken:
- Season the chicken breasts with salt and black pepper.
- Spread a generous layer of pesto over each chicken breast.
- In a shallow dish, combine the grated Parmesan cheese and breadcrumbs (if using).
- Press the pesto-coated side of each chicken breast into the Parmesan mixture, ensuring an even coating.

Cook the Chicken:
- Place the chicken breasts on a baking sheet lined with parchment paper.
- Bake in the preheated oven for about 20-25 minutes or until the chicken is cooked through and the crust is golden brown.

Prepare the Brussels Sprouts:
- While the chicken is baking, toss the halved Brussels sprouts with olive oil, salt, and black pepper.
- Spread the Brussels sprouts on a separate baking sheet.

Roast Brussels Sprouts:

- Place the Brussels sprouts in the oven alongside the chicken during the last 15-20 minutes of cooking, or until they are tender and slightly crispy on the edges.

Serve:
- Once the chicken and Brussels sprouts are done, remove them from the oven.
- Serve the Pesto Parmesan Crusted Chicken on a plate alongside the roasted Brussels sprouts.

Garnish (Optional):
- Garnish with additional grated Parmesan cheese and fresh chopped basil or parsley for extra flavor.

Enjoy your Pesto Parmesan Crusted Chicken with Brussels Sprouts! This dish pairs well with a side of pasta, rice, or a simple green salad.

BBQ Ranch Chicken Drumsticks with Sweet Potato Wedges

Ingredients:

For the Chicken Drumsticks:

- 8-10 chicken drumsticks
- Salt and black pepper, to taste
- 1 cup barbecue sauce
- 1/2 cup ranch dressing
- 1 teaspoon smoked paprika (optional, for extra smokiness)

For the Sweet Potato Wedges:

- 2 large sweet potatoes, washed and cut into wedges
- 2 tablespoons olive oil
- 1 teaspoon garlic powder
- 1 teaspoon paprika
- Salt and black pepper, to taste

Instructions:

Preheat the Oven:

- Preheat your oven to 425°F (220°C).
- Prepare the Chicken Drumsticks:
    - Season the chicken drumsticks with salt and black pepper.
    - In a bowl, mix together barbecue sauce, ranch dressing, and smoked paprika (if using).
    - Coat the drumsticks with the barbecue ranch mixture, making sure they are well coated.
- Prepare the Sweet Potato Wedges:
    - In a separate bowl, toss the sweet potato wedges with olive oil, garlic powder, paprika, salt, and black pepper until evenly coated.
- Arrange on Baking Sheets:
    - Place the chicken drumsticks on a baking sheet lined with parchment paper, ensuring they are not too crowded to allow even cooking.

- Spread the sweet potato wedges on a separate baking sheet.

Bake in the Oven:
- Bake both the chicken drumsticks and sweet potato wedges in the preheated oven.
- Bake the sweet potato wedges for about 25-30 minutes or until they are golden and tender.
- Bake the chicken drumsticks for about 35-40 minutes or until they reach an internal temperature of 165°F (74°C), and the skin is crispy.

Serve:
- Arrange the BBQ Ranch Chicken Drumsticks on a serving platter alongside the sweet potato wedges.

Garnish (Optional):
- Garnish with chopped fresh parsley or green onions for a burst of color and freshness.

Serve this delicious dish with additional barbecue sauce and ranch dressing on the side for dipping. Enjoy your BBQ Ranch Chicken Drumsticks with Sweet Potato Wedges!

Sheet Pan Fajitas with Steak and Bell Peppers

Ingredients:

- 1.5 pounds flank steak, thinly sliced
- 3 bell peppers (assorted colors), sliced
- 1 large red onion, thinly sliced
- 3 tablespoons olive oil
- 1 teaspoon chili powder
- 1 teaspoon cumin
- 1 teaspoon paprika
- 1 teaspoon garlic powder
- 1 teaspoon onion powder
- 1/2 teaspoon cayenne pepper (adjust to taste)
- Salt and black pepper, to taste
- Juice of 1 lime
- Fresh cilantro, chopped (for garnish)
- Flour tortillas, for serving

Instructions:

Preheat the Oven:

    Preheat your oven to 400°F (200°C).
    Prepare the Steak and Vegetables:
- Place the sliced flank steak, bell peppers, and red onion on a large baking sheet.
- Drizzle olive oil over the steak and vegetables.
- Sprinkle chili powder, cumin, paprika, garlic powder, onion powder, cayenne pepper, salt, and black pepper evenly over the steak and vegetables.

    Toss and Coat:
- Use your hands or tongs to toss everything together, ensuring the steak and vegetables are well coated with the oil and seasonings.

    Arrange on the Baking Sheet:
- Spread the steak and vegetables in an even layer on the baking sheet, avoiding overcrowding for even cooking.

    Bake in the Oven:

- Bake in the preheated oven for 15-20 minutes or until the steak is cooked to your desired level of doneness and the vegetables are tender, stirring once or twice during cooking.

Finish and Serve:
- Squeeze the lime juice over the cooked fajita mixture.
- Garnish with chopped fresh cilantro.
- Warm the flour tortillas according to the package instructions.

Assemble Fajitas:
- Serve the steak and bell peppers on warm tortillas.
- Add your favorite toppings such as salsa, guacamole, sour cream, or shredded cheese.

Enjoy your Sheet Pan Fajitas with Steak and Bell Peppers for a delicious and hassle-free meal!

Harissa Roasted Vegetables with Spiced Chicken Thighs

Ingredients:

For the Spiced Chicken Thighs:

- 4-6 bone-in, skin-on chicken thighs
- 2 tablespoons harissa paste
- 1 teaspoon ground cumin
- 1 teaspoon ground coriander
- 1 teaspoon smoked paprika
- Salt and black pepper, to taste
- 2 tablespoons olive oil

For the Harissa Roasted Vegetables:

- 1 pound baby potatoes, halved
- 2 carrots, peeled and sliced into rounds
- 1 red bell pepper, sliced
- 1 yellow bell pepper, sliced
- 1 red onion, thinly sliced
- 3 tablespoons harissa paste
- 2 tablespoons olive oil
- 1 teaspoon ground cumin
- 1 teaspoon ground coriander
- Salt and black pepper, to taste

Instructions:

Preheat the Oven:

Preheat your oven to 400°F (200°C).
Prepare the Chicken Thighs:
- In a bowl, mix harissa paste, ground cumin, ground coriander, smoked paprika, salt, black pepper, and olive oil.
- Coat the chicken thighs with the harissa spice mixture, ensuring they are well covered.

Prepare the Vegetables:
- In a large bowl, combine the baby potatoes, carrots, red bell pepper, yellow bell pepper, red onion, harissa paste, olive oil, ground cumin, ground coriander, salt, and black pepper.
- Toss until the vegetables are evenly coated with the harissa mixture.

Arrange on Baking Sheets:
- Place the spiced chicken thighs on one side of a large baking sheet.
- Spread the harissa-coated vegetables on the other side of the baking sheet, ensuring everything is in a single layer.

Roast in the Oven:
- Roast in the preheated oven for about 40-45 minutes or until the chicken is cooked through and the vegetables are tender, stirring the vegetables once or twice during cooking.

Serve:
- Arrange the spiced chicken thighs on a serving platter alongside the harissa roasted vegetables.

Garnish (Optional):
- Garnish with fresh chopped cilantro or parsley for a burst of freshness.

Enjoy your Harissa Roasted Vegetables with Spiced Chicken Thighs! This dish can be served as is or with a side of couscous or rice for a complete meal.

Maple Dijon Glazed Pork Chops with Brussels Sprouts

Ingredients:

For the Maple Dijon Glazed Pork Chops:

- 4 bone-in pork chops
- Salt and black pepper, to taste
- 1/4 cup Dijon mustard
- 1/4 cup pure maple syrup
- 2 tablespoons olive oil
- 2 cloves garlic, minced
- 1 teaspoon dried thyme or 1 tablespoon fresh thyme leaves

For the Brussels Sprouts:

- 1 pound Brussels sprouts, trimmed and halved
- 2 tablespoons olive oil
- Salt and black pepper, to taste
- Optional: Balsamic glaze for drizzling (for serving)

Instructions:

Preheat the Oven:

Preheat your oven to 400°F (200°C).
Season Pork Chops:
- Season the pork chops with salt and black pepper on both sides.

Prepare Maple Dijon Glaze:
- In a small bowl, whisk together Dijon mustard, maple syrup, olive oil, minced garlic, and thyme.

Coat Pork Chops:
- Brush the pork chops with the maple Dijon glaze, making sure to coat them on both sides.

Prepare Brussels Sprouts:
- In a separate bowl, toss the halved Brussels sprouts with olive oil, salt, and black pepper.

Arrange on Baking Sheet:
- Place the glazed pork chops on a baking sheet lined with parchment paper.
- Spread the Brussels sprouts around the pork chops.

Roast in the Oven:
- Roast in the preheated oven for about 25-30 minutes or until the pork chops reach an internal temperature of 145°F (63°C) and the Brussels sprouts are golden brown and tender.

Broil (Optional):
- If you want a caramelized finish, you can broil the pork chops for an additional 2-3 minutes, keeping a close eye to prevent burning.

Serve:
- Transfer the glazed pork chops and roasted Brussels sprouts to a serving platter.
- Drizzle any remaining glaze over the pork chops.
- Optionally, drizzle balsamic glaze over the Brussels sprouts for added flavor.

Enjoy your Maple Dijon Glazed Pork Chops with Brussels Sprouts! Serve with your favorite side dishes, such as mashed potatoes or quinoa.

Cajun Shrimp and Sausage with Okra

Ingredients:

- 1 pound large shrimp, peeled and deveined
- 1/2 pound smoked sausage, sliced
- 1 pound fresh okra, trimmed and sliced
- 1 onion, diced
- 1 bell pepper, diced
- 3 celery stalks, diced
- 3 cloves garlic, minced
- 2 tablespoons Cajun seasoning (adjust to taste)
- 1 teaspoon paprika
- 1 teaspoon dried thyme
- 1 teaspoon dried oregano
- 1/2 teaspoon cayenne pepper (optional, for extra heat)
- Salt and black pepper, to taste
- 2 tablespoons olive oil
- 1 can (14 ounces) diced tomatoes
- 1 cup chicken broth
- Cooked rice, for serving

Instructions:

   Prep Ingredients:
- Peel and devein the shrimp.
- Slice the smoked sausage.
- Trim and slice the fresh okra.
- Dice the onion, bell pepper, and celery.
- Mince the garlic.

   Season Shrimp:
- In a bowl, toss the shrimp with Cajun seasoning, paprika, dried thyme, dried oregano, cayenne pepper (if using), salt, and black pepper. Set aside.

   Sauté Vegetables:
- In a large skillet or pan, heat olive oil over medium-high heat.
- Add diced onion, bell pepper, and celery. Sauté until the vegetables are softened.

   Add Sausage and Okra:

- Add sliced smoked sausage and okra to the skillet. Cook for a few minutes until the sausage is browned and the okra starts to soften.

Add Garlic and Cajun Seasoning:
- Stir in minced garlic and Cajun seasoning. Cook for another minute until the garlic becomes fragrant.

Cook Shrimp:
- Add seasoned shrimp to the skillet and cook until they turn pink, about 2-3 minutes.

Add Tomatoes and Broth:
- Pour in the diced tomatoes and chicken broth. Stir well to combine.

Simmer:
- Allow the mixture to simmer for about 10-15 minutes, letting the flavors meld together and the sauce thicken.

Adjust Seasoning:
- Taste and adjust the seasoning if necessary. Add more Cajun seasoning, salt, or black pepper to suit your preference.

Serve:
- Serve the Cajun Shrimp and Sausage with Okra over cooked rice.

Enjoy your spicy and delicious Cajun-inspired meal! This dish is perfect for those who love bold flavors and a bit of heat.

Greek Lemon Chicken with Potatoes and Green Beans

Ingredients:

For the Lemon Chicken:

- 4 bone-in, skin-on chicken thighs
- Salt and black pepper, to taste
- 1 teaspoon dried oregano
- 1 teaspoon dried thyme
- 4 cloves garlic, minced
- Zest of 1 lemon
- Juice of 2 lemons
- 3 tablespoons olive oil

For the Potatoes and Green Beans:

- 1.5 pounds baby potatoes, halved
- 1 pound green beans, trimmed
- 2 tablespoons olive oil
- Salt and black pepper, to taste
- 1 teaspoon dried oregano
- 1 teaspoon garlic powder

Instructions:

Preheat the Oven:

Preheat your oven to 400°F (200°C).
Season Chicken:
- Pat the chicken thighs dry with paper towels.
- Season both sides of the chicken thighs with salt, black pepper, dried oregano, and dried thyme.

Prepare Lemon Mixture:
- In a bowl, mix minced garlic, lemon zest, lemon juice, and olive oil.

Marinate Chicken:
- Place the chicken thighs in a large bowl or resealable plastic bag.

- Pour the lemon mixture over the chicken, making sure each piece is well-coated.
- Marinate for at least 30 minutes, or refrigerate for a few hours for better flavor.

Prepare Potatoes and Green Beans:
- In a separate bowl, toss halved baby potatoes and trimmed green beans with olive oil, salt, black pepper, dried oregano, and garlic powder.

Arrange on Baking Sheet:
- Place the marinated chicken thighs on a baking sheet lined with parchment paper, skin side up.
- Surround the chicken with the seasoned potatoes and green beans.

Roast in the Oven:
- Roast in the preheated oven for about 40-45 minutes or until the chicken is cooked through, and the potatoes are tender, stirring the vegetables halfway through cooking.

Broil (Optional):
- If you want a crispy skin on the chicken, you can broil for an additional 2-3 minutes, keeping a close eye to prevent burning.

Serve:
- Transfer the Greek Lemon Chicken, Potatoes, and Green Beans to a serving platter.

Garnish (Optional):
- Garnish with fresh chopped parsley and additional lemon wedges for serving.

Serve this delicious dish with a side of Tzatziki sauce or a Greek salad for a complete and satisfying meal. Enjoy your Greek Lemon Chicken with Potatoes and Green Beans!

Italian Sausage with Peppers, Onions, and Potatoes

Ingredients:

- 1.5 pounds Italian sausage links (sweet or hot), cut into thirds
- 1 pound baby potatoes, halved or quartered
- 2 bell peppers, sliced (use a mix of colors for variety)
- 1 large onion, sliced
- 3 cloves garlic, minced
- 2 tablespoons olive oil
- 1 teaspoon dried oregano
- 1 teaspoon dried thyme
- 1 teaspoon dried rosemary
- Salt and black pepper, to taste
- Red pepper flakes (optional, for added heat)
- Fresh parsley, chopped (for garnish)

Instructions:

Preheat the Oven:

  Preheat your oven to 400°F (200°C).
  Prepare Vegetables:
  - In a large bowl, toss the halved baby potatoes, sliced bell peppers, sliced onions, and minced garlic with olive oil, dried oregano, dried thyme, dried rosemary, salt, black pepper, and red pepper flakes (if using).
  Arrange on Baking Sheet:
  - Spread the seasoned vegetables on a baking sheet lined with parchment paper.
  Add Sausage:
  - Nestle the cut Italian sausage pieces among the vegetables on the baking sheet.
  Roast in the Oven:
  - Roast in the preheated oven for about 30-35 minutes or until the sausage is cooked through, and the vegetables are tender, stirring halfway through to ensure even cooking.
  Broil (Optional):

- If you want a bit of char on the sausages and vegetables, you can broil for an additional 2-3 minutes, keeping a close eye to prevent burning.

Serve:
- Transfer the Italian Sausage, Peppers, Onions, and Potatoes to a serving platter.

Garnish (Optional):
- Garnish with fresh chopped parsley for a burst of color and freshness.

Enjoy your Italian Sausage with Peppers, Onions, and Potatoes! This dish is delicious on its own or served with a side of crusty bread or a simple green salad.

Orange Glazed Salmon with Asparagus and Broccolini

Ingredients:

For the Orange Glazed Salmon:

- 4 salmon fillets
- Salt and black pepper, to taste
- 1/4 cup orange juice
- Zest of 1 orange
- 2 tablespoons soy sauce (or tamari for a gluten-free option)
- 2 tablespoons honey or maple syrup
- 2 cloves garlic, minced
- 1 teaspoon grated fresh ginger
- 1 tablespoon olive oil

For the Asparagus and Broccolini:

- 1 bunch asparagus, tough ends trimmed
- 1 bunch broccolini, ends trimmed
- 2 tablespoons olive oil
- Salt and black pepper, to taste
- Crushed red pepper flakes (optional, for added heat)
- Sesame seeds, for garnish
- Sliced green onions, for garnish

Instructions:

Preheat the Oven:

> Preheat your oven to 400°F (200°C).
> Prepare the Orange Glazed Salmon:
> - Season the salmon fillets with salt and black pepper. Place them in a shallow dish.
>
> Make the Glaze:
> - In a small bowl, whisk together orange juice, orange zest, soy sauce, honey (or maple syrup), minced garlic, and grated ginger.

Marinate Salmon:
- Pour half of the orange glaze over the salmon fillets, reserving the remaining glaze for later. Allow the salmon to marinate for about 15-20 minutes.

Roast Salmon:
- Heat olive oil in an oven-safe skillet over medium-high heat. Sear the salmon fillets for 2-3 minutes on each side, then transfer the skillet to the preheated oven and roast for an additional 10-12 minutes or until the salmon is cooked to your liking.

Prepare Asparagus and Broccolini:
- While the salmon is roasting, toss the trimmed asparagus and broccolini with olive oil, salt, black pepper, and crushed red pepper flakes (if using).

Roast Vegetables:
- Spread the seasoned asparagus and broccolini on a baking sheet and roast in the oven for about 10-12 minutes or until they are tender but still crisp.

Serve:
- Arrange the roasted Orange Glazed Salmon on plates alongside the asparagus and broccolini.

Drizzle Glaze and Garnish:
- Drizzle the remaining orange glaze over the salmon.
- Garnish with sesame seeds and sliced green onions.

Enjoy your Orange Glazed Salmon with Asparagus and Broccolini! This dish is not only delicious but also visually appealing with vibrant colors and flavors.

Sheet Pan Teriyaki Beef and Broccoli

Ingredients:

For the Teriyaki Sauce:

- 1/2 cup soy sauce
- 1/4 cup water
- 3 tablespoons honey
- 2 tablespoons rice vinegar
- 1 tablespoon sesame oil
- 1 tablespoon grated fresh ginger
- 2 cloves garlic, minced
- 1 tablespoon cornstarch mixed with 2 tablespoons water (optional, for thickening)

For the Beef and Broccoli:

- 1.5 pounds flank steak, thinly sliced
- 1 head broccoli, cut into florets
- 1 red bell pepper, sliced
- 1 yellow bell pepper, sliced
- 2 tablespoons vegetable oil
- Salt and black pepper, to taste
- Sesame seeds and chopped green onions, for garnish (optional)
- Cooked white or brown rice, for serving

Instructions:

Preheat the Oven:

    Preheat your oven to 425°F (220°C).
    Make Teriyaki Sauce:
- In a small saucepan, combine soy sauce, water, honey, rice vinegar, sesame oil, grated ginger, and minced garlic. Bring to a simmer over medium heat.
- If you want a thicker sauce, add the cornstarch-water mixture and stir until the sauce thickens. Set aside.

    Prepare Beef and Vegetables:

- Place the thinly sliced flank steak, broccoli florets, and sliced bell peppers on a large baking sheet.

Season and Toss:
- Drizzle the vegetable oil over the beef and vegetables.
- Season with salt and black pepper to taste.
- Toss everything on the baking sheet to coat evenly with oil and seasoning.

Pour Teriyaki Sauce:
- Pour half of the teriyaki sauce over the beef and vegetables, reserving the remaining half for later.

Roast in the Oven:
- Roast in the preheated oven for about 15-20 minutes or until the beef is cooked to your liking, and the vegetables are tender-crisp. You can stir once or twice during cooking for even coating.

Serve:
- Remove from the oven and drizzle the remaining teriyaki sauce over the beef and vegetables.

Garnish (Optional):
- Garnish with sesame seeds and chopped green onions.
- Serve over cooked rice.

Enjoy your Sheet Pan Teriyaki Beef and Broccoli! This dish is not only tasty but also makes cleanup a breeze since it's all cooked on one pan.

Lemon Herb Butter Baked Cod with Zucchini

Ingredients:

For the Lemon Herb Butter:

- 1/2 cup (1 stick) unsalted butter, softened
- 2 tablespoons fresh lemon juice
- 2 teaspoons lemon zest
- 2 tablespoons chopped fresh parsley
- 1 tablespoon chopped fresh dill
- 1 clove garlic, minced
- Salt and black pepper, to taste

For the Baked Cod and Zucchini:

- 4 cod fillets
- Salt and black pepper, to taste
- 2 medium zucchini, sliced into rounds or half-moons
- Olive oil, for drizzling
- Lemon slices, for garnish (optional)
- Fresh parsley, for garnish

Instructions:

Preheat the Oven:

    Preheat your oven to 400°F (200°C).
    Prepare Lemon Herb Butter:
- In a bowl, combine softened butter, fresh lemon juice, lemon zest, chopped parsley, chopped dill, minced garlic, salt, and black pepper. Mix well until all ingredients are incorporated.

    Season Cod and Zucchini:
- Pat the cod fillets dry with a paper towel and season both sides with salt and black pepper.
- Place the sliced zucchini in a bowl, drizzle with olive oil, and season with salt and black pepper. Toss to coat.

    Assemble on Baking Sheet:

- Line a baking sheet with parchment paper. Place the seasoned cod fillets on one side of the baking sheet and arrange the zucchini slices on the other side.

Top with Lemon Herb Butter:
- Spread a generous portion of the lemon herb butter over each cod fillet. Reserve some butter for drizzling over the zucchini.

Bake in the Oven:
- Bake in the preheated oven for about 15-20 minutes or until the cod is cooked through and easily flakes with a fork. The zucchini should be tender.

Drizzle with Remaining Herb Butter:
- Once out of the oven, drizzle the remaining lemon herb butter over the baked zucchini.

Garnish and Serve:
- Garnish with lemon slices and fresh parsley.
- Serve the Lemon Herb Butter Baked Cod with Zucchini over a bed of rice or with your favorite side dish.

Enjoy this light and delightful dish with the bright flavors of lemon and fresh herbs!

Herb Crusted Pork Tenderloin with Carrots and Potatoes

Ingredients:

For the Herb Crust:

- 1 1/2 pounds pork tenderloin
- Salt and black pepper, to taste
- 2 tablespoons Dijon mustard
- 2 tablespoons olive oil
- 2 cloves garlic, minced
- 1 tablespoon fresh rosemary, chopped
- 1 tablespoon fresh thyme, chopped
- 1 tablespoon fresh parsley, chopped
- 1 tablespoon fresh sage, chopped (optional)

For the Roasted Vegetables:

- 1 pound baby potatoes, halved or quartered
- 1 pound baby carrots, or peeled and sliced carrots
- 2 tablespoons olive oil
- Salt and black pepper, to taste
- 1 teaspoon dried thyme (or use fresh if available)

Instructions:

Preheat the Oven:

Preheat your oven to 425°F (220°C).

Prepare Pork Tenderloin:
- Pat the pork tenderloin dry with paper towels.
- Season with salt and black pepper.

Make Herb Crust:
- In a bowl, mix together Dijon mustard, olive oil, minced garlic, chopped rosemary, thyme, parsley, and sage (if using). This creates a herb paste.
- Rub the herb paste all over the pork tenderloin, ensuring it's evenly coated.

Prepare Vegetables:
- In a separate bowl, toss the halved or quartered baby potatoes and baby carrots with olive oil, salt, black pepper, and dried thyme.

Arrange on Baking Sheet:

- Place the herb-crusted pork tenderloin in the center of a baking sheet lined with parchment paper.
- Arrange the seasoned vegetables around the pork.

Roast in the Oven:
- Roast in the preheated oven for about 25-30 minutes or until the internal temperature of the pork reaches 145°F (63°C) and the vegetables are tender, stirring the vegetables halfway through for even cooking.

Rest and Slice:
- Let the pork rest for a few minutes before slicing it into medallions.

Serve:
- Arrange the sliced herb-crusted pork tenderloin on a serving platter alongside the roasted vegetables.

Garnish (Optional):
- Garnish with additional fresh herbs, if desired.

Enjoy your Herb-Crusted Pork Tenderloin with Carrots and Potatoes! This dish makes for a satisfying and flavorful meal perfect for family dinners or special occasions.

Mediterranean Veggie Bake with Chickpeas

Ingredients:

- 1 can (15 ounces) chickpeas, drained and rinsed
- 1 large eggplant, diced
- 1 zucchini, diced
- 1 red bell pepper, diced
- 1 yellow bell pepper, diced
- 1 pint cherry tomatoes, halved
- 1 red onion, thinly sliced
- 3 cloves garlic, minced
- 1/4 cup extra-virgin olive oil
- 1 teaspoon dried oregano
- 1 teaspoon dried thyme
- 1 teaspoon dried rosemary
- Salt and black pepper, to taste
- 1/2 cup crumbled feta cheese (optional, for garnish)
- Fresh parsley, chopped (for garnish)
- Lemon wedges (for serving)

Instructions:

Preheat the Oven:

Preheat your oven to 400°F (200°C).
Prepare Vegetables and Chickpeas:
- In a large mixing bowl, combine diced eggplant, zucchini, red bell pepper, yellow bell pepper, cherry tomatoes, red onion, and chickpeas.

Season:
- Drizzle the vegetables and chickpeas with olive oil.
- Add minced garlic, dried oregano, dried thyme, dried rosemary, salt, and black pepper. Toss until everything is well coated.

Bake:
- Spread the mixture evenly on a baking sheet lined with parchment paper.

Roast in the Oven:

- Roast in the preheated oven for about 30-35 minutes or until the vegetables are tender and slightly caramelized, stirring once or twice during cooking.

Garnish and Serve:
- Once out of the oven, garnish with crumbled feta cheese (if using) and fresh chopped parsley.

Serve:
- Serve the Mediterranean Veggie Bake with Chickpeas on a platter.
- Optionally, serve with lemon wedges on the side for a burst of citrus flavor.

Enjoy your Mediterranean Veggie Bake with Chickpeas as a main dish or as a delightful side. This dish is versatile and can be served over couscous, quinoa, or with a side of crusty bread.

Maple Mustard Glazed Chicken Thighs with Brussels Sprouts

Ingredients:

For the Maple Mustard Glaze:

- 1/4 cup Dijon mustard
- 2 tablespoons whole grain mustard
- 3 tablespoons maple syrup
- 2 tablespoons soy sauce
- 2 cloves garlic, minced
- 1 teaspoon dried thyme (or 1 tablespoon fresh thyme leaves)
- Salt and black pepper, to taste

For the Chicken Thighs and Brussels Sprouts:

- 4-6 bone-in, skin-on chicken thighs
- 1 pound Brussels sprouts, trimmed and halved
- 2 tablespoons olive oil
- Salt and black pepper, to taste
- 1 tablespoon balsamic glaze (optional, for drizzling)
- Fresh parsley, chopped (for garnish)

Instructions:

Preheat the Oven:

    Preheat your oven to 425°F (220°C).
    Make the Maple Mustard Glaze:
- In a bowl, whisk together Dijon mustard, whole grain mustard, maple syrup, soy sauce, minced garlic, dried thyme, salt, and black pepper. Set aside.

    Prepare Chicken Thighs:
- Pat the chicken thighs dry with paper towels.
- Season with salt and black pepper on both sides.

    Prepare Brussels Sprouts:
- Toss the halved Brussels sprouts with olive oil, salt, and black pepper.

Arrange on Baking Sheet:
- Place the chicken thighs on a baking sheet lined with parchment paper.
- Surround the chicken with the seasoned Brussels sprouts.

Brush with Maple Mustard Glaze:
- Brush the chicken thighs with the maple mustard glaze, ensuring they are well coated.
- Reserve some glaze for later.

Roast in the Oven:
- Roast in the preheated oven for about 30-35 minutes or until the chicken is cooked through, and the skin is crispy, stirring the Brussels sprouts once or twice during cooking.

Broil (Optional):
- If you want a caramelized finish, you can broil the chicken for an additional 2-3 minutes, keeping a close eye to prevent burning.

Finish and Serve:
- Drizzle the remaining maple mustard glaze over the chicken and Brussels sprouts.
- Optionally, drizzle balsamic glaze over the Brussels sprouts for added flavor.

Garnish:
- Garnish with chopped fresh parsley.

Enjoy your Maple Mustard Glazed Chicken Thighs with Brussels Sprouts! This dish pairs well with rice, quinoa, or a side of roasted sweet potatoes.

Sheet Pan Garlic Butter Shrimp with Asparagus

Ingredients:

- 1 pound large shrimp, peeled and deveined
- 1 bunch asparagus, trimmed
- 4 tablespoons unsalted butter, melted
- 4 cloves garlic, minced
- 1 teaspoon paprika
- 1/2 teaspoon crushed red pepper flakes (optional, for heat)
- Salt and black pepper, to taste
- 1 lemon, sliced
- Fresh parsley, chopped (for garnish)

Instructions:

Preheat the Oven:

    Preheat your oven to 400°F (200°C).
    Prepare Shrimp and Asparagus:
- In a large bowl, combine the peeled and deveined shrimp with trimmed asparagus.

    Make Garlic Butter Mixture:
- In a small bowl, mix together melted butter, minced garlic, paprika, crushed red pepper flakes (if using), salt, and black pepper.

    Coat Shrimp and Asparagus:
- Pour the garlic butter mixture over the shrimp and asparagus. Toss to coat them evenly.

    Arrange on Baking Sheet:
- Spread the shrimp and asparagus on a baking sheet in a single layer.

    Bake in the Oven:
- Bake in the preheated oven for about 12-15 minutes or until the shrimp are opaque and the asparagus is tender, stirring once halfway through.

    Broil (Optional):
- If you want a bit of char on the shrimp, you can broil for an additional 2-3 minutes, keeping a close eye to prevent burning.

    Garnish and Serve:

- Remove from the oven and garnish with sliced lemons and chopped fresh parsley.

Serve:
- Serve the Sheet Pan Garlic Butter Shrimp with Asparagus as is or over cooked rice, pasta, or quinoa.

Enjoy your easy and delicious Sheet Pan Garlic Butter Shrimp with Asparagus! This dish is perfect for a quick weeknight dinner or a simple yet impressive meal.

Teriyaki Salmon with Snap Peas and Red Onion

Ingredients:

For the Teriyaki Sauce:

- 1/4 cup soy sauce
- 2 tablespoons mirin
- 2 tablespoons sake or dry white wine
- 2 tablespoons brown sugar
- 1 tablespoon honey
- 1 teaspoon sesame oil
- 2 cloves garlic, minced
- 1 teaspoon grated fresh ginger
- 1 tablespoon cornstarch mixed with 2 tablespoons water (optional, for thickening)

For the Salmon and Vegetables:

- 4 salmon fillets
- Salt and black pepper, to taste
- 1 pound snap peas, trimmed
- 1 medium red onion, thinly sliced
- 2 tablespoons vegetable oil
- Sesame seeds, for garnish
- Sliced green onions, for garnish
- Cooked rice, for serving

Instructions:

Preheat the Oven:

> Preheat your oven to 400°F (200°C).
> Make Teriyaki Sauce:
> - In a small saucepan, combine soy sauce, mirin, sake (or white wine), brown sugar, honey, sesame oil, minced garlic, and grated ginger. Bring to a simmer over medium heat.

- If you want a thicker sauce, add the cornstarch-water mixture and stir until the sauce thickens. Set aside.

Prepare Salmon:
- Pat the salmon fillets dry with paper towels.
- Season with salt and black pepper on both sides.

Prepare Snap Peas and Red Onion:
- In a large bowl, toss the trimmed snap peas and thinly sliced red onion with vegetable oil.

Assemble on Baking Sheet:
- Place the seasoned salmon fillets on a baking sheet lined with parchment paper.
- Surround the salmon with the snap peas and red onion.

Brush with Teriyaki Sauce:
- Brush the salmon fillets and vegetables with the prepared teriyaki sauce, reserving some for later.

Roast in the Oven:
- Roast in the preheated oven for about 15-18 minutes or until the salmon is cooked through and the vegetables are crisp-tender.

Garnish:
- Drizzle the remaining teriyaki sauce over the salmon and vegetables.
- Garnish with sesame seeds and sliced green onions.

Serve:
- Serve the Teriyaki Salmon with Snap Peas and Red Onion over cooked rice.

Enjoy your Teriyaki Salmon with a perfect balance of sweetness and umami, complemented by the crispness of snap peas and the vibrant color of red onion!

Herb Roasted Turkey Breast with Fall Vegetables

Ingredients:

For the Turkey Breast:

- 1 whole turkey breast (bone-in and skin-on), about 4-5 pounds
- 2 tablespoons olive oil
- 2 cloves garlic, minced
- 1 tablespoon fresh thyme, chopped
- 1 tablespoon fresh rosemary, chopped
- 1 tablespoon fresh sage, chopped
- Salt and black pepper, to taste

For the Fall Vegetables:

- 1 pound baby potatoes, halved or quartered
- 2 medium sweet potatoes, peeled and diced
- 2 carrots, peeled and sliced
- 1 red onion, cut into wedges
- 2 tablespoons olive oil
- Salt and black pepper, to taste
- 1 teaspoon dried thyme
- 1 teaspoon paprika
- 1/2 teaspoon ground cinnamon

Instructions:

Preheat the Oven:

Preheat your oven to 375°F (190°C).

Prepare the Turkey Breast:
- Rinse the turkey breast and pat it dry with paper towels.
- In a small bowl, mix together olive oil, minced garlic, chopped thyme, rosemary, sage, salt, and black pepper.
- Rub the herb mixture all over the turkey breast, ensuring it's well coated.

Prepare the Fall Vegetables:
- In a large mixing bowl, toss the halved or quartered baby potatoes, diced sweet potatoes, sliced carrots, and red onion wedges with olive oil, salt, black pepper, dried thyme, paprika, and ground cinnamon.

Assemble on Baking Sheet:
- Place the herb-rubbed turkey breast in the center of a baking sheet lined with parchment paper.
- Arrange the seasoned fall vegetables around the turkey.

Roast in the Oven:
- Roast in the preheated oven for about 1 to 1.5 hours or until the turkey reaches an internal temperature of 165°F (74°C) and the vegetables are tender, stirring the vegetables once or twice during cooking.

Rest and Slice:
- Allow the turkey to rest for about 10 minutes before slicing it into thin slices.

Serve:
- Arrange the Herb-Roasted Turkey Breast slices on a serving platter alongside the fall vegetables.

Garnish (Optional):
- Garnish with additional fresh herbs, if desired.

Enjoy your Herb-Roasted Turkey Breast with Fall Vegetables! This dish is perfect for a festive fall or Thanksgiving dinner, bringing warmth and delicious flavors to the table.

Honey Garlic Chicken Thighs with Brussels Sprouts

Ingredients:

For the Honey Garlic Chicken Thighs:

- 4 bone-in, skin-on chicken thighs
- Salt and black pepper, to taste
- 3 tablespoons honey
- 3 tablespoons soy sauce
- 3 cloves garlic, minced
- 1 teaspoon ginger, grated
- 1 tablespoon olive oil

For the Brussels Sprouts:

- 1 pound Brussels sprouts, trimmed and halved
- 2 tablespoons olive oil
- Salt and black pepper, to taste
- Crushed red pepper flakes (optional, for added heat)

Instructions:

Preheat the Oven:

    Preheat your oven to 400°F (200°C).
    Prepare Chicken Thighs:
- Pat the chicken thighs dry with paper towels.
- Season both sides with salt and black pepper.

    Make Honey Garlic Sauce:
- In a small bowl, whisk together honey, soy sauce, minced garlic, and grated ginger.

    Coat Chicken Thighs:
- Brush the chicken thighs with the honey garlic sauce, coating them thoroughly.

    Prepare Brussels Sprouts:

- In a large mixing bowl, toss the halved Brussels sprouts with olive oil, salt, black pepper, and optional crushed red pepper flakes.

Arrange on Baking Sheet:
- Place the honey garlic-coated chicken thighs on one side of a baking sheet lined with parchment paper.
- Spread the seasoned Brussels sprouts on the other side.

Roast in the Oven:
- Roast in the preheated oven for about 30-35 minutes or until the chicken is cooked through and the Brussels sprouts are golden brown and crispy, stirring the Brussels sprouts halfway through for even cooking.

Broil (Optional):
- If you desire a crispier skin on the chicken, you can broil for an additional 2-3 minutes, keeping a close eye to prevent burning.

Serve:
- Transfer the Honey Garlic Chicken Thighs and Brussels Sprouts to a serving platter.

Garnish (Optional):
- Drizzle any remaining honey garlic sauce over the chicken.
- Garnish with fresh chopped parsley or green onions for a burst of freshness.

Enjoy your Honey Garlic Chicken Thighs with Brussels Sprouts! This dish is a perfect balance of sweet and savory, with a touch of caramelization on the chicken and a delightful crispiness on the Brussels sprouts.

Lemon Butter Baked Tilapia with Roasted Vegetables

Ingredients:

For the Lemon Butter Baked Tilapia:

- 4 tilapia fillets
- Salt and black pepper, to taste
- 2 tablespoons unsalted butter, melted
- 2 tablespoons fresh lemon juice
- 1 teaspoon lemon zest
- 2 cloves garlic, minced
- 1 teaspoon dried oregano
- 1 teaspoon dried thyme
- 1/2 teaspoon paprika
- Fresh parsley, chopped (for garnish)
- Lemon slices (for serving)

For the Roasted Vegetables:

- 1 pound baby potatoes, halved or quartered
- 1 large carrot, peeled and sliced
- 1 zucchini, sliced
- 1 red bell pepper, sliced
- 1 tablespoon olive oil
- Salt and black pepper, to taste
- 1 teaspoon dried rosemary
- 1 teaspoon dried thyme

Instructions:

Preheat the Oven:

Preheat your oven to 400°F (200°C).
Prepare Tilapia Fillets:
- Pat the tilapia fillets dry with paper towels.
- Season with salt and black pepper on both sides.

Make Lemon Butter Mixture:
- In a small bowl, whisk together melted butter, fresh lemon juice, lemon zest, minced garlic, dried oregano, dried thyme, and paprika.

Coat Tilapia:
- Place the tilapia fillets on a baking sheet lined with parchment paper.
- Brush the fillets with the lemon butter mixture, ensuring they are well coated.

Prepare Roasted Vegetables:
- In a separate bowl, toss the halved or quartered baby potatoes, sliced carrot, zucchini, and red bell pepper with olive oil, salt, black pepper, dried rosemary, and dried thyme.

Arrange on Baking Sheet:
- Spread the seasoned vegetables around the tilapia fillets on the baking sheet.

Bake in the Oven:
- Bake in the preheated oven for about 15-20 minutes or until the tilapia is cooked through and flakes easily with a fork, and the vegetables are tender and golden.

Garnish and Serve:
- Garnish the Lemon Butter Baked Tilapia with chopped fresh parsley.
- Serve with lemon slices on the side.

Enjoy your Lemon Butter Baked Tilapia with Roasted Vegetables! This dish is not only delicious but also a wholesome and well-balanced meal.

Sheet Pan Pesto Chicken with Cherry Tomatoes and Mozzarella

Ingredients:

- 4 boneless, skinless chicken breasts
- Salt and black pepper, to taste
- 1 cup cherry tomatoes, halved
- 1 cup fresh mozzarella balls, halved
- 1/3 cup basil pesto (store-bought or homemade)
- 2 tablespoons olive oil
- 2 cloves garlic, minced
- Fresh basil, chopped (for garnish)
- Balsamic glaze (optional, for drizzling)

Instructions:

Preheat the Oven:

Preheat your oven to 400°F (200°C).

Prepare Chicken Breasts:
- Pat the chicken breasts dry with paper towels.
- Season both sides with salt and black pepper.

Assemble on Baking Sheet:
- Place the seasoned chicken breasts on a baking sheet lined with parchment paper.

Prepare Pesto Mixture:
- In a small bowl, mix together the basil pesto, olive oil, and minced garlic.

Coat Chicken with Pesto:
- Brush the chicken breasts with the pesto mixture, ensuring they are well coated.

Add Tomatoes and Mozzarella:
- Scatter the halved cherry tomatoes and mozzarella balls around the chicken on the baking sheet.

Bake in the Oven:
- Bake in the preheated oven for about 20-25 minutes or until the chicken is cooked through, and the tomatoes and mozzarella are slightly golden and bubbly.

Broil (Optional):

- If you want a golden crust on the cheese, you can broil for an additional 2-3 minutes, keeping a close eye to prevent burning.

Garnish and Serve:
- Garnish the Sheet Pan Pesto Chicken with chopped fresh basil.
- Optionally, drizzle with balsamic glaze for extra flavor.

Serve:
- Serve the Pesto Chicken with Cherry Tomatoes and Mozzarella over cooked pasta, rice, or a bed of mixed greens.

Enjoy your Sheet Pan Pesto Chicken with Cherry Tomatoes and Mozzarella! This dish is not only visually appealing but also bursting with the flavors of summer.

Chipotle Lime Chicken with Corn and Black Beans

Ingredients:

For the Chipotle Lime Chicken:

- 4 boneless, skinless chicken breasts
- Salt and black pepper, to taste
- 2 tablespoons olive oil
- 2 chipotle peppers in adobo sauce, minced
- 3 tablespoons adobo sauce (from the chipotle pepper can)
- Juice of 2 limes
- 2 teaspoons ground cumin
- 1 teaspoon garlic powder
- 1 teaspoon onion powder
- 1 teaspoon dried oregano

For the Corn and Black Bean Salsa:

- 1 can (15 ounces) black beans, drained and rinsed
- 1 cup corn kernels (fresh, frozen, or canned)
- 1 red bell pepper, diced
- 1/2 red onion, finely diced
- 1/4 cup fresh cilantro, chopped
- Juice of 1 lime
- Salt and black pepper, to taste

Instructions:

Preheat the Grill or Oven:
- Preheat your grill or oven to medium-high heat.

Prepare Chipotle Lime Marinade:
- In a small bowl, whisk together olive oil, minced chipotle peppers, adobo sauce, lime juice, ground cumin, garlic powder, onion powder, dried oregano, salt, and black pepper.

Marinate Chicken:
- Season the chicken breasts with salt and black pepper.

- Place the chicken in a large zip-top bag and pour half of the chipotle lime marinade over the chicken. Seal the bag and let it marinate for at least 30 minutes.

Prepare Corn and Black Bean Salsa:
- In a bowl, combine black beans, corn, diced red bell pepper, finely diced red onion, chopped cilantro, lime juice, salt, and black pepper. Mix well and set aside.

Grill or Bake Chicken:
- Grill the marinated chicken breasts for about 6-8 minutes per side or until they reach an internal temperature of 165°F (74°C). Alternatively, you can bake them in the oven at 400°F (200°C) for approximately 20-25 minutes.

Rest and Slice:
- Allow the grilled or baked chicken to rest for a few minutes before slicing it into strips.

Serve:
- Serve the Chipotle Lime Chicken strips over a bed of the Corn and Black Bean Salsa.

Garnish (Optional):
- Garnish with additional fresh cilantro and lime wedges if desired.

Enjoy your Chipotle Lime Chicken with Corn and Black Beans! This dish is not only delicious but also a perfect balance of spicy, smoky, and citrusy flavors.

Teriyaki Tofu and Broccoli for a vegetarian option

Ingredients:

For the Teriyaki Sauce:

- 1/2 cup soy sauce
- 3 tablespoons mirin (sweet rice wine)
- 2 tablespoons rice vinegar
- 2 tablespoons brown sugar
- 1 tablespoon sesame oil
- 1 tablespoon cornstarch mixed with 2 tablespoons water (optional, for thickening)

For the Tofu and Broccoli:

- 1 block firm or extra-firm tofu, pressed and cubed
- 3 cups broccoli florets
- 2 tablespoons vegetable oil
- 3 cloves garlic, minced
- 1 tablespoon fresh ginger, grated
- Sesame seeds, for garnish
- Green onions, chopped, for garnish
- Cooked rice, for serving

Instructions:

Prepare the Teriyaki Sauce:
- In a small saucepan, combine soy sauce, mirin, rice vinegar, brown sugar, and sesame oil. Bring to a simmer over medium heat.
- If you want a thicker sauce, add the cornstarch-water mixture and stir until the sauce thickens. Set aside.

Prepare Tofu:
- Press the tofu to remove excess water. Cut it into cubes.

Cook Tofu and Broccoli:
- Heat vegetable oil in a large skillet or wok over medium-high heat.
- Add tofu cubes and cook until they become golden brown on all sides.

- Add minced garlic and grated ginger to the skillet. Stir-fry for about 1-2 minutes until fragrant.
- Add broccoli florets and continue stir-frying for an additional 3-4 minutes or until the broccoli is tender but still crisp.

Add Teriyaki Sauce:
- Pour the prepared teriyaki sauce over the tofu and broccoli.
- Gently toss everything to coat evenly. Allow the sauce to simmer for an additional 2-3 minutes.

Serve:
- Serve Teriyaki Tofu and Broccoli over cooked rice.

Garnish:
- Garnish with sesame seeds and chopped green onions.

Enjoy your Teriyaki Tofu and Broccoli! This vegetarian dish is a tasty and satisfying alternative, and the teriyaki sauce adds a perfect balance of sweet and savory flavors.

Lemon Rosemary Roasted Cornish Hens with Root Vegetables

Ingredients:

For the Cornish Hens:

- 2 Cornish hens, about 1.5 to 2 pounds each
- Salt and black pepper, to taste
- 2 tablespoons olive oil
- Zest of 1 lemon
- 2 tablespoons fresh lemon juice
- 2 tablespoons fresh rosemary, chopped
- 4 cloves garlic, minced

For the Root Vegetables:

- 1 pound baby potatoes, halved
- 2 carrots, peeled and cut into chunks
- 2 parsnips, peeled and cut into chunks
- 1 sweet potato, peeled and cut into chunks
- 1 red onion, cut into wedges
- 3 tablespoons olive oil
- Salt and black pepper, to taste
- 1 teaspoon dried thyme

Instructions:

Preheat the Oven:

Preheat your oven to 425°F (220°C).
Prepare Cornish Hens:
- Pat the Cornish hens dry with paper towels.
- Season the hens inside and out with salt and black pepper.

Make Lemon Rosemary Mixture:
- In a small bowl, combine olive oil, lemon zest, lemon juice, chopped rosemary, and minced garlic.

Coat Cornish Hens:

- Rub the lemon rosemary mixture all over the Cornish hens, making sure to coat them evenly.

Prepare Root Vegetables:
- In a large mixing bowl, toss the halved baby potatoes, carrot chunks, parsnip chunks, sweet potato chunks, and red onion wedges with olive oil, salt, black pepper, and dried thyme.

Assemble on Baking Sheet:
- Place the seasoned Cornish hens in the center of a baking sheet lined with parchment paper.
- Arrange the seasoned root vegetables around the hens.

Roast in the Oven:
- Roast in the preheated oven for about 50-60 minutes or until the hens are golden brown and cooked through, and the vegetables are tender, stirring the vegetables once or twice during cooking.

Rest and Serve:
- Allow the Cornish hens to rest for a few minutes before serving.

Garnish (Optional):
- Garnish with additional fresh rosemary and lemon slices if desired.

Serve:
- Serve the Lemon Rosemary Roasted Cornish Hens with Root Vegetables on a platter.

Enjoy your elegant and flavorful Lemon Rosemary Roasted Cornish Hens with a side of deliciously roasted root vegetables!

Sheet Pan Caprese Chicken with Balsamic Glaze

Ingredients:

- 4 boneless, skinless chicken breasts
- Salt and black pepper, to taste
- 2 tablespoons olive oil
- 4 tablespoons balsamic glaze (store-bought or homemade)
- 1 teaspoon dried oregano
- 1 teaspoon dried basil
- 1 pint cherry tomatoes, halved
- 8 ounces fresh mozzarella balls, halved
- Fresh basil leaves, for garnish
- Balsamic glaze, for drizzling

Instructions:

Preheat the Oven:

Preheat your oven to 400°F (200°C).
Prepare Chicken Breasts:
- Pat the chicken breasts dry with paper towels.
- Season both sides with salt and black pepper.

Coat Chicken with Olive Oil:
- Place the chicken breasts on a baking sheet lined with parchment paper.
- Brush both sides of the chicken with olive oil.

Season and Bake:
- Sprinkle dried oregano and dried basil evenly over the chicken breasts.
- Bake in the preheated oven for about 20-25 minutes or until the chicken is cooked through.

Add Tomatoes and Mozzarella:
- About 5 minutes before the chicken is done, remove the baking sheet from the oven.
- Scatter the halved cherry tomatoes and fresh mozzarella balls around the chicken.

Return to Oven:
- Return the baking sheet to the oven and bake for an additional 5-7 minutes or until the cheese is melted, and the tomatoes are slightly softened.

Garnish:

- Garnish the Sheet Pan Caprese Chicken with fresh basil leaves.

Drizzle with Balsamic Glaze:
- Drizzle balsamic glaze over the chicken, tomatoes, and mozzarella.

Serve:
- Serve the Caprese Chicken over a bed of cooked pasta, rice, or with a side of crusty bread.

Enjoy your Sheet Pan Caprese Chicken with Balsamic Glaze, a delightful and flavorful meal that's perfect for a quick weeknight dinner or a casual gathering.

Spicy Maple Glazed Salmon with Sweet Potato Wedges

Ingredients:

For the Spicy Maple Glazed Salmon:

- 4 salmon fillets
- Salt and black pepper, to taste
- 2 tablespoons maple syrup
- 1 tablespoon soy sauce
- 1 tablespoon Dijon mustard
- 1 tablespoon olive oil
- 1 teaspoon chili powder (adjust to taste)
- 1/2 teaspoon smoked paprika
- 1/2 teaspoon garlic powder
- 1/4 teaspoon cayenne pepper (adjust to taste)

For the Sweet Potato Wedges:

- 2 large sweet potatoes, peeled and cut into wedges
- 2 tablespoons olive oil
- 1 teaspoon smoked paprika
- 1 teaspoon cumin
- Salt and black pepper, to taste

Instructions:

Preheat the Oven:

>Preheat your oven to 400°F (200°C).
>Prepare Sweet Potato Wedges:
>- In a large bowl, toss the sweet potato wedges with olive oil, smoked paprika, cumin, salt, and black pepper until evenly coated.
>
>Arrange on Baking Sheet:
>- Place the seasoned sweet potato wedges on a baking sheet lined with parchment paper in a single layer.
>
>Bake Sweet Potatoes:
>- Bake in the preheated oven for about 25-30 minutes or until the sweet potatoes are tender and golden, turning them once halfway through.
>
>Prepare Spicy Maple Glazed Salmon:

- In a small bowl, whisk together maple syrup, soy sauce, Dijon mustard, olive oil, chili powder, smoked paprika, garlic powder, cayenne pepper, salt, and black pepper.

Coat Salmon Fillets:
- Place the salmon fillets on the baking sheet with the sweet potatoes.
- Brush the spicy maple glaze over the salmon fillets, ensuring they are well coated.

Bake Salmon and Sweet Potatoes:
- Bake for an additional 12-15 minutes or until the salmon is cooked through and flakes easily with a fork.

Broil (Optional):
- If you want a caramelized finish, you can broil the salmon for an additional 2-3 minutes, keeping a close eye to prevent burning.

Serve:
- Serve the Spicy Maple Glazed Salmon with Sweet Potato Wedges.

Enjoy your Spicy Maple Glazed Salmon with Sweet Potato Wedges, a delightful and balanced meal that brings together sweet, savory, and spicy flavors!

Herb Roasted Chicken Drumsticks with Cauliflower

Ingredients:

For the Herb-Roasted Chicken Drumsticks:

- 8 chicken drumsticks
- 2 tablespoons olive oil
- 2 teaspoons dried thyme
- 2 teaspoons dried rosemary
- 2 teaspoons dried oregano
- 1 teaspoon garlic powder
- 1 teaspoon onion powder
- Salt and black pepper, to taste
- Lemon wedges (for serving)

For the Roasted Cauliflower:

- 1 large head of cauliflower, cut into florets
- 3 tablespoons olive oil
- 2 teaspoons smoked paprika
- 1 teaspoon ground cumin
- Salt and black pepper, to taste
- Fresh parsley, chopped (for garnish)

Instructions:

Preheat the Oven:

> Preheat your oven to 425°F (220°C).
> Prepare Chicken Drumsticks:
> - In a large bowl, toss the chicken drumsticks with olive oil, dried thyme, dried rosemary, dried oregano, garlic powder, onion powder, salt, and black pepper until well coated.
>
> Assemble on Baking Sheet:
> - Place the seasoned chicken drumsticks on a baking sheet lined with parchment paper in a single layer.

Prepare Cauliflower:
- In a separate bowl, toss the cauliflower florets with olive oil, smoked paprika, ground cumin, salt, and black pepper until evenly coated.

Assemble on Baking Sheet:
- Arrange the seasoned cauliflower around the chicken drumsticks on the baking sheet.

Roast in the Oven:
- Roast in the preheated oven for about 35-40 minutes or until the chicken is golden brown and cooked through, and the cauliflower is tender and slightly caramelized.

Check Doneness:
- Ensure the internal temperature of the chicken reaches 165°F (74°C).

Garnish and Serve:
- Garnish with chopped fresh parsley.
- Serve the Herb-Roasted Chicken Drumsticks with Roasted Cauliflower on a platter with lemon wedges on the side.

Enjoy your Herb-Roasted Chicken Drumsticks with Cauliflower, a wholesome and flavorful dish that's perfect for a family dinner or a casual get-together!

Lemon Garlic Butter Shrimp with Asparagus

Ingredients:

- 1 pound large shrimp, peeled and deveined
- Salt and black pepper, to taste
- 2 tablespoons olive oil
- 3 tablespoons unsalted butter
- 4 cloves garlic, minced
- 1 bunch asparagus, tough ends trimmed and spears cut into bite-sized pieces
- Zest of 1 lemon
- Juice of 1 lemon
- 1/2 cup chicken broth or white wine (optional)
- Fresh parsley, chopped (for garnish)
- Lemon wedges (for serving)

Instructions:

Season Shrimp:
- Pat the shrimp dry with paper towels and season with salt and black pepper.

Cook Shrimp:
- In a large skillet, heat olive oil over medium-high heat.
- Add shrimp to the skillet and cook for 1-2 minutes per side or until they start to turn pink. Remove the shrimp from the skillet and set aside.

Sauté Asparagus:
- In the same skillet, add 2 tablespoons of unsalted butter.
- Add minced garlic and sauté for about 30 seconds until fragrant.
- Add the asparagus pieces to the skillet and cook for 3-4 minutes or until they are crisp-tender.

Make Lemon Garlic Butter Sauce:
- Return the cooked shrimp to the skillet.
- Add the remaining 1 tablespoon of butter, lemon zest, and lemon juice.
- If using, pour in the chicken broth or white wine for extra flavor.

Combine and Simmer:
- Toss everything together in the skillet and let it simmer for an additional 2-3 minutes, allowing the flavors to meld and the sauce to thicken slightly.

Check Seasoning:

- Taste and adjust the seasoning with additional salt and black pepper if needed.

Garnish and Serve:
- Garnish with chopped fresh parsley.
- Serve the Lemon Garlic Butter Shrimp with Asparagus over cooked pasta, rice, or with a side of crusty bread.
- Optionally, serve with lemon wedges for an extra burst of citrus flavor.

Enjoy your Lemon Garlic Butter Shrimp with Asparagus, a delicious and light meal that's perfect for a quick weeknight dinner or a special occasion!

Baked Greek Chicken with Artichokes and Kalamata Olives

Ingredients:

- 4 boneless, skinless chicken breasts
- Salt and black pepper, to taste
- 2 tablespoons olive oil
- 4 cloves garlic, minced
- 1 teaspoon dried oregano
- 1 teaspoon dried thyme
- 1 teaspoon dried rosemary
- 1 teaspoon dried basil
- 1/2 teaspoon paprika
- 1/2 teaspoon onion powder
- 1/4 teaspoon red pepper flakes (optional, for heat)
- 1 can (14 ounces) artichoke hearts, drained and halved
- 1 cup Kalamata olives, pitted
- 1 cup cherry tomatoes, halved
- 1/2 cup crumbled feta cheese
- Fresh parsley, chopped (for garnish)
- Lemon wedges (for serving)

Instructions:

Preheat the Oven:

Preheat your oven to 375°F (190°C).
Prepare Chicken Breasts:
- Pat the chicken breasts dry with paper towels.
- Season both sides with salt and black pepper.

Create Greek Seasoning Mixture:
- In a small bowl, mix together olive oil, minced garlic, dried oregano, dried thyme, dried rosemary, dried basil, paprika, onion powder, and red pepper flakes (if using).

Coat Chicken:
- Brush the chicken breasts with the Greek seasoning mixture, ensuring they are well coated.

Assemble in Baking Dish:

- Place the seasoned chicken breasts in a baking dish.

Add Artichokes, Olives, and Tomatoes:
- Scatter the halved artichoke hearts, Kalamata olives, and cherry tomato halves around the chicken.

Bake in the Oven:
- Bake in the preheated oven for about 25-30 minutes or until the chicken is cooked through, and the vegetables are tender.

Top with Feta Cheese:
- Sprinkle crumbled feta cheese over the top of the chicken and vegetables during the last 5 minutes of baking, allowing it to melt slightly.

Garnish and Serve:
- Garnish the Baked Greek Chicken with Artichokes and Kalamata Olives with chopped fresh parsley.
- Serve with lemon wedges on the side for squeezing over the dish.

Enjoy your Baked Greek Chicken with Artichokes and Kalamata Olives! This dish is not only delicious but also a colorful and vibrant addition to your Mediterranean-inspired meals.

Cajun Roasted Sausage and Vegetables

Ingredients:

- 1 pound smoked sausage (andouille or your preferred type), sliced
- 1 pound baby potatoes, halved
- 1 bell pepper, sliced
- 1 red onion, sliced
- 1 zucchini, sliced
- 1 yellow squash, sliced
- 1 cup cherry tomatoes
- 3 tablespoons olive oil
- 2 tablespoons Cajun seasoning
- 1 teaspoon garlic powder
- 1 teaspoon onion powder
- 1/2 teaspoon paprika
- 1/2 teaspoon dried thyme
- 1/4 teaspoon cayenne pepper (adjust to taste)
- Salt and black pepper, to taste
- Fresh parsley, chopped (for garnish, optional)

Instructions:

Preheat the Oven:

> Preheat your oven to 400°F (200°C).
> Prepare Vegetables and Sausage:
> - In a large mixing bowl, combine the sliced sausage, halved baby potatoes, sliced bell pepper, sliced red onion, sliced zucchini, sliced yellow squash, and cherry tomatoes.
>
> Make Cajun Seasoning Mixture:
> - In a small bowl, mix together olive oil, Cajun seasoning, garlic powder, onion powder, paprika, dried thyme, cayenne pepper, salt, and black pepper.
>
> Coat Vegetables and Sausage:
> - Pour the Cajun seasoning mixture over the sausage and vegetables.
> - Toss everything together until the sausage and vegetables are evenly coated.

Arrange on Baking Sheet:
- Spread the seasoned sausage and vegetables in a single layer on a baking sheet lined with parchment paper.

Roast in the Oven:
- Roast in the preheated oven for about 25-30 minutes or until the sausage is cooked through, and the vegetables are tender and slightly caramelized, stirring halfway through for even cooking.

Garnish and Serve:
- If desired, garnish the Cajun Roasted Sausage and Vegetables with chopped fresh parsley.

Serve:
- Serve the dish as is or over cooked rice, quinoa, or a bed of greens.

Enjoy your Cajun Roasted Sausage and Vegetables! This dish is a delightful mix of bold flavors and textures, making it a satisfying and comforting meal.

Mediterranean Baked Cod with Feta and Tomatoes

Ingredients:

- 4 cod fillets
- Salt and black pepper, to taste
- 2 tablespoons olive oil
- 4 cloves garlic, minced
- 1 can (14 ounces) diced tomatoes, drained
- 1/2 cup Kalamata olives, pitted and sliced
- 1 teaspoon dried oregano
- 1 teaspoon dried basil
- 1 teaspoon dried thyme
- 1/2 teaspoon red pepper flakes (optional, for heat)
- 1 cup crumbled feta cheese
- Fresh parsley, chopped (for garnish)
- Lemon wedges (for serving)

Instructions:

Preheat the Oven:

Preheat your oven to 375°F (190°C).

Prepare Cod Fillets:
- Pat the cod fillets dry with paper towels.
- Season both sides with salt and black pepper.

Sauté Garlic and Tomatoes:
- In an oven-safe skillet, heat olive oil over medium heat.
- Add minced garlic and sauté for about 30 seconds until fragrant.
- Add diced tomatoes, sliced Kalamata olives, dried oregano, dried basil, dried thyme, and red pepper flakes (if using).
- Cook for 2-3 minutes, allowing the flavors to meld.

Place Cod in Skillet:
- Place the seasoned cod fillets in the skillet, nestling them into the tomato mixture.

Bake in the Oven:
- Transfer the skillet to the preheated oven and bake for about 15-20 minutes or until the cod is cooked through and flakes easily with a fork.

Add Feta Cheese:

- Sprinkle crumbled feta cheese evenly over the top of the cod and tomato mixture.

Broil (Optional):
- If you want a golden crust on the feta, you can broil the skillet for an additional 2-3 minutes, keeping a close eye to prevent burning.

Garnish and Serve:
- Garnish the Mediterranean Baked Cod with Feta and Tomatoes with chopped fresh parsley.
- Serve with lemon wedges on the side for squeezing over the cod.

Enjoy your Mediterranean Baked Cod with Feta and Tomatoes, a delightful and healthy dish inspired by the flavors of the Mediterranean!

Pesto Ranch Chicken Thighs with Brussels Sprouts

Ingredients:

For the Pesto Ranch Chicken Thighs:

- 6 bone-in, skin-on chicken thighs
- Salt and black pepper, to taste
- 1/3 cup basil pesto (store-bought or homemade)
- 2 tablespoons ranch seasoning mix (store-bought or homemade)
- 2 tablespoons olive oil

For the Brussels Sprouts:

- 1 pound Brussels sprouts, trimmed and halved
- 2 tablespoons olive oil
- Salt and black pepper, to taste

Instructions:

Preheat the Oven:

Preheat your oven to 400°F (200°C).
Prepare Chicken Thighs:
- Pat the chicken thighs dry with paper towels.
- Season both sides with salt and black pepper.

Combine Pesto and Ranch:
- In a small bowl, mix together the basil pesto, ranch seasoning mix, and olive oil to create a marinade.

Coat Chicken Thighs:
- Brush the chicken thighs with the pesto ranch marinade, ensuring they are well coated.

Prepare Brussels Sprouts:
- In a separate bowl, toss the halved Brussels sprouts with olive oil, salt, and black pepper.

Assemble on Baking Sheet:

- Place the marinated chicken thighs on a baking sheet lined with parchment paper, skin side up.
- Scatter the seasoned Brussels sprouts around the chicken.

Bake in the Oven:
- Bake in the preheated oven for about 30-35 minutes or until the chicken thighs are cooked through, and the skin is golden and crispy.

Check Doneness:
- Ensure the internal temperature of the chicken reaches 165°F (74°C).

Broil (Optional):
- If you desire a crispier skin, you can broil the chicken for an additional 2-3 minutes, keeping a close eye to prevent burning.

Serve:
- Serve the Pesto Ranch Chicken Thighs with Brussels Sprouts on a platter.

Enjoy your Pesto Ranch Chicken Thighs with Brussels Sprouts, a delicious and comforting meal with the perfect blend of herby and savory flavors!

Sesame Ginger Glazed Salmon with Broccoli

Ingredients:

For the Sesame Ginger Glaze:

- 1/4 cup soy sauce
- 2 tablespoons rice vinegar
- 2 tablespoons honey
- 1 tablespoon sesame oil
- 1 tablespoon fresh ginger, grated
- 2 cloves garlic, minced
- 1 tablespoon sesame seeds (for garnish)
- Red pepper flakes (optional, for heat)

For the Salmon and Broccoli:

- 4 salmon fillets
- Salt and black pepper, to taste
- 1 pound broccoli florets
- 2 tablespoons olive oil
- Green onions, sliced (for garnish)
- Cooked white or brown rice (for serving)

Instructions:

Preheat the Oven:

    Preheat your oven to 400°F (200°C).
    Prepare Sesame Ginger Glaze:
- In a small bowl, whisk together soy sauce, rice vinegar, honey, sesame oil, grated ginger, minced garlic, and red pepper flakes (if using). Set aside.

    Prepare Salmon and Broccoli:
- Pat the salmon fillets dry with paper towels and season with salt and black pepper.
- In a large mixing bowl, toss the broccoli florets with olive oil and season with salt.

Assemble on Baking Sheet:
- Place the seasoned salmon fillets on a baking sheet lined with parchment paper.
- Arrange the broccoli around the salmon.

Brush with Sesame Ginger Glaze:
- Brush the salmon fillets and broccoli with the sesame ginger glaze, reserving some for later.

Bake in the Oven:
- Bake in the preheated oven for about 15-20 minutes or until the salmon is cooked through, and the broccoli is tender-crisp.

Broil (Optional):
- If you desire a caramelized finish, you can broil the salmon and broccoli for an additional 2-3 minutes, keeping a close eye to prevent burning.

Garnish and Serve:
- Drizzle the remaining sesame ginger glaze over the salmon and broccoli.
- Garnish with sesame seeds and sliced green onions.

Serve:
- Serve the Sesame Ginger Glazed Salmon with Broccoli over cooked rice.

Enjoy your Sesame Ginger Glazed Salmon with Broccoli, a delicious and nutrient-packed meal that's perfect for a quick and wholesome dinner!

BBQ Ranch Chicken and Potatoes

Ingredients:

For the BBQ Ranch Marinade:

- 1/2 cup barbecue sauce
- 1/4 cup ranch dressing
- 2 tablespoons olive oil
- 2 teaspoons smoked paprika
- 1 teaspoon garlic powder
- 1 teaspoon onion powder
- Salt and black pepper, to taste

For the Chicken and Potatoes:

- 4 bone-in, skin-on chicken thighs
- 4 medium-sized potatoes, diced
- 2 tablespoons olive oil
- Salt and black pepper, to taste
- Fresh parsley, chopped (for garnish, optional)
- Ranch dressing (for serving, optional)

Instructions:

Preheat the Oven:

    Preheat your oven to 425°F (220°C).
    Prepare BBQ Ranch Marinade:
- In a bowl, whisk together barbecue sauce, ranch dressing, olive oil, smoked paprika, garlic powder, onion powder, salt, and black pepper to create the marinade.

    Marinate Chicken:
- Place the chicken thighs in a resealable plastic bag or a shallow dish.
- Pour half of the BBQ Ranch marinade over the chicken, ensuring it's well-coated.

- Allow the chicken to marinate in the refrigerator for at least 30 minutes, or preferably, up to 4 hours.

Prepare Potatoes:
- In a separate bowl, toss the diced potatoes with olive oil, salt, and black pepper.

Assemble on Baking Sheet:
- Place the marinated chicken thighs on a baking sheet lined with parchment paper, skin side up.
- Arrange the seasoned potatoes around the chicken.

Bake in the Oven:
- Bake in the preheated oven for about 35-40 minutes or until the chicken is cooked through and the potatoes are golden and crispy, turning the potatoes once or twice during cooking.

Check Doneness:
- Ensure the internal temperature of the chicken reaches 165°F (74°C).

Garnish and Serve:
- Garnish with chopped fresh parsley if desired.
- Serve the BBQ Ranch Chicken and Potatoes hot.
- Drizzle with additional ranch dressing before serving, if desired.

Enjoy your BBQ Ranch Chicken and Potatoes, a satisfying and flavorful meal that's perfect for a family dinner or a casual get-together!

Spicy Maple Glazed Chicken Drumsticks with Brussels Sprouts

Ingredients:

For the Spicy Maple Glaze:

- 1/4 cup maple syrup
- 2 tablespoons soy sauce
- 1 tablespoon Dijon mustard
- 1 tablespoon Sriracha sauce (adjust to taste)
- 1 tablespoon olive oil
- 2 cloves garlic, minced
- Salt and black pepper, to taste

For the Chicken Drumsticks and Brussels Sprouts:

- 12 chicken drumsticks
- 1 pound Brussels sprouts, trimmed and halved
- 2 tablespoons olive oil
- Salt and black pepper, to taste
- Sesame seeds (for garnish, optional)
- Green onions, sliced (for garnish, optional)

Instructions:

Preheat the Oven:

    Preheat your oven to 400°F (200°C).
    Prepare Spicy Maple Glaze:
- In a small saucepan over medium heat, combine maple syrup, soy sauce, Dijon mustard, Sriracha sauce, olive oil, minced garlic, salt, and black pepper.
- Bring the mixture to a simmer, stirring constantly.
- Reduce heat and let it simmer for 2-3 minutes until the glaze thickens slightly.
- Remove from heat and set aside.

    Prepare Chicken Drumsticks and Brussels Sprouts:

- In a large mixing bowl, toss the chicken drumsticks with olive oil, salt, and black pepper until well coated.
- Place the drumsticks on one side of a baking sheet lined with parchment paper.
- In the same bowl, toss the halved Brussels sprouts with olive oil, salt, and black pepper.
- Arrange the Brussels sprouts on the other side of the baking sheet.

Brush with Spicy Maple Glaze:
- Brush the chicken drumsticks with the spicy maple glaze, reserving some for later.
- Toss the Brussels sprouts with a portion of the glaze.

Bake in the Oven:
- Bake in the preheated oven for about 35-40 minutes or until the chicken is cooked through, and the Brussels sprouts are golden and crispy, turning the drumsticks and stirring the Brussels sprouts halfway through.

Broil (Optional):
- If you want a caramelized finish, you can broil the drumsticks and Brussels sprouts for an additional 2-3 minutes, keeping a close eye to prevent burning.

Garnish and Serve:
- Drizzle the remaining spicy maple glaze over the drumsticks and Brussels sprouts.
- Garnish with sesame seeds and sliced green onions if desired.

Serve:
- Serve the Spicy Maple Glazed Chicken Drumsticks with Brussels Sprouts hot.

Enjoy your Spicy Maple Glazed Chicken Drumsticks with Brussels Sprouts, a delightful and flavorful meal that's perfect for a weeknight dinner or a casual gathering!

Lemon Herb Sheet Pan Pork Chops with Green Beans

Ingredients:

For the Lemon Herb Marinade:

- 1/4 cup olive oil
- Zest of 1 lemon
- Juice of 1 lemon
- 2 cloves garlic, minced
- 1 teaspoon dried thyme
- 1 teaspoon dried rosemary
- 1 teaspoon dried oregano
- Salt and black pepper, to taste

For the Pork Chops and Green Beans:

- 4 bone-in pork chops
- 1 pound fresh green beans, trimmed
- 2 tablespoons olive oil
- Salt and black pepper, to taste
- Lemon slices (for garnish, optional)
- Fresh parsley, chopped (for garnish, optional)

Instructions:

Preheat the Oven:

    Preheat your oven to 400°F (200°C).
    Prepare Lemon Herb Marinade:
- In a small bowl, whisk together olive oil, lemon zest, lemon juice, minced garlic, dried thyme, dried rosemary, dried oregano, salt, and black pepper.

    Marinate Pork Chops:
- Place the pork chops in a resealable plastic bag or a shallow dish.
- Pour the lemon herb marinade over the pork chops, ensuring they are well coated.
- Allow the pork chops to marinate in the refrigerator for at least 30 minutes, or preferably, up to 4 hours.

    Prepare Green Beans:

- In a large mixing bowl, toss the trimmed green beans with olive oil, salt, and black pepper until evenly coated.

Assemble on Baking Sheet:
- Place the marinated pork chops on a baking sheet lined with parchment paper.
- Arrange the green beans around the pork chops.

Roast in the Oven:
- Roast in the preheated oven for about 25-30 minutes or until the pork chops are cooked through, and the green beans are tender-crisp, turning the pork chops and stirring the green beans halfway through.

Check Doneness:
- Ensure the internal temperature of the pork chops reaches 145°F (63°C).

Garnish and Serve:
- Garnish the Lemon Herb Sheet Pan Pork Chops with Green Beans with lemon slices and chopped fresh parsley if desired.

Serve:
- Serve the pork chops and green beans hot.

Enjoy your Lemon Herb Sheet Pan Pork Chops with Green Beans, a delightful and well-balanced meal that's perfect for a quick and wholesome dinner!

Mediterranean Chickpea and Eggplant Bake

Ingredients:

- 1 large eggplant, diced
- 1 can (15 ounces) chickpeas, drained and rinsed
- 1 cup cherry tomatoes, halved
- 1 red onion, finely chopped
- 3 cloves garlic, minced
- 1/4 cup olive oil
- 1 teaspoon dried oregano
- 1 teaspoon dried thyme
- 1 teaspoon smoked paprika
- Salt and black pepper, to taste
- 1/2 cup crumbled feta cheese
- Fresh parsley, chopped (for garnish)

Instructions:

Preheat the Oven:

Preheat your oven to 400°F (200°C).

Prepare Vegetables:

- In a large mixing bowl, combine the diced eggplant, drained chickpeas, halved cherry tomatoes, chopped red onion, and minced garlic.

Season with Herbs and Spices:

- Drizzle the olive oil over the vegetables.
- Add dried oregano, dried thyme, smoked paprika, salt, and black pepper to taste.
- Toss everything together until the vegetables are well coated with the seasoning.

Assemble in Baking Dish:

- Transfer the seasoned vegetables to a baking dish, spreading them out in an even layer.

Roast in the Oven:

- Roast in the preheated oven for about 30-35 minutes or until the eggplant is tender and the chickpeas are crispy, stirring halfway through for even cooking.

Check Doneness:

- Taste and adjust the seasoning if needed.

Add Feta Cheese:
- Sprinkle the crumbled feta cheese over the top of the baked chickpea and eggplant mixture during the last 5 minutes of baking, allowing it to melt slightly.

Garnish and Serve:
- Garnish the Mediterranean Chickpea and Eggplant Bake with chopped fresh parsley.

Serve:
- Serve the dish as a side or as a main course with crusty bread or over cooked quinoa.

Enjoy your Mediterranean Chickpea and Eggplant Bake, a flavorful and hearty dish inspired by the delicious flavors of the Mediterranean!

Orange Glazed Chicken Thighs with Carrots and Broccoli

Ingredients:

For the Orange Glaze:

- 1/2 cup orange juice (freshly squeezed if possible)
- Zest of 1 orange
- 3 tablespoons soy sauce
- 2 tablespoons honey
- 1 tablespoon rice vinegar
- 1 teaspoon fresh ginger, grated
- 2 cloves garlic, minced
- 1 teaspoon cornstarch (optional, for thickening)
- Red pepper flakes (optional, for heat)
- Salt and black pepper, to taste

For the Chicken Thighs and Vegetables:

- 6 bone-in, skin-on chicken thighs
- 1 pound baby carrots, peeled
- 1 pound broccoli florets
- 2 tablespoons olive oil
- Salt and black pepper, to taste
- Sesame seeds (for garnish, optional)
- Green onions, sliced (for garnish, optional)

Instructions:

Preheat the Oven:

    Preheat your oven to 400°F (200°C).
    Prepare Orange Glaze:
- In a small saucepan over medium heat, combine orange juice, orange zest, soy sauce, honey, rice vinegar, grated ginger, minced garlic, and red pepper flakes (if using).
- Bring the mixture to a simmer, stirring occasionally.

- If you want a thicker glaze, dissolve cornstarch in a tablespoon of water and stir it into the sauce. Simmer until the glaze thickens slightly.
- Season with salt and black pepper to taste. Set aside.

Prepare Chicken Thighs and Vegetables:
- Pat the chicken thighs dry with paper towels.
- In a large mixing bowl, toss the chicken thighs, baby carrots, and broccoli florets with olive oil, salt, and black pepper until well coated.

Assemble in Baking Dish:
- Place the chicken thighs, carrots, and broccoli in a baking dish in a single layer.

Brush with Orange Glaze:
- Brush the chicken thighs and vegetables with the prepared orange glaze, reserving some for later.

Roast in the Oven:
- Roast in the preheated oven for about 30-35 minutes or until the chicken is cooked through and the vegetables are tender, basting with the remaining orange glaze halfway through.

Check Doneness:
- Ensure the internal temperature of the chicken reaches 165°F (74°C).

Garnish and Serve:
- Garnish the Orange Glazed Chicken Thighs with Carrots and Broccoli with sesame seeds and sliced green onions if desired.

Serve:
- Serve the dish hot, with additional orange glaze on the side for drizzling.

Enjoy your Orange Glazed Chicken Thighs with Carrots and Broccoli, a delightful and citrus-infused meal that's perfect for a family dinner or a special occasion!

Sheet Pan Shrimp Scampi with Asparagus

Ingredients:

- 1 pound large shrimp, peeled and deveined
- 1 bunch asparagus, tough ends trimmed
- 4 tablespoons unsalted butter, melted
- 4 cloves garlic, minced
- Zest of 1 lemon
- Juice of 1 lemon
- 2 tablespoons chopped fresh parsley
- Salt and black pepper, to taste
- Red pepper flakes (optional, for heat)
- 2 tablespoons olive oil
- Lemon wedges (for serving)

Instructions:

Preheat the Oven:

Preheat your oven to 400°F (200°C).
Prepare Shrimp and Asparagus:
- Pat the shrimp dry with paper towels.
- In a large mixing bowl, toss the shrimp and trimmed asparagus with melted butter, minced garlic, lemon zest, lemon juice, chopped fresh parsley, salt, black pepper, and red pepper flakes (if using).

Assemble on Baking Sheet:
- Spread the shrimp and asparagus in a single layer on a baking sheet lined with parchment paper.

Drizzle with Olive Oil:
- Drizzle the olive oil over the shrimp and asparagus.

Roast in the Oven:
- Roast in the preheated oven for about 12-15 minutes or until the shrimp are pink and opaque, and the asparagus is tender-crisp. Be cautious not to overcook the shrimp.

Broil (Optional):
- If you desire a slightly charred finish, you can broil the sheet pan for an additional 1-2 minutes, keeping a close eye to prevent burning.

Check Seasoning:
- Taste and adjust the seasoning with additional salt, pepper, or red pepper flakes if needed.

Garnish and Serve:
- Garnish the Sheet Pan Shrimp Scampi with Asparagus with additional chopped parsley.
- Serve hot with lemon wedges on the side for squeezing over the shrimp.

Enjoy your Sheet Pan Shrimp Scampi with Asparagus, a flavorful and hassle-free meal that's perfect for a quick weeknight dinner!

Hoisin Glazed Sheet Pan Pork with Cabbage

Ingredients:

For the Hoisin Glaze:

- 1/4 cup hoisin sauce
- 2 tablespoons soy sauce
- 2 tablespoons honey
- 1 tablespoon rice vinegar
- 1 tablespoon sesame oil
- 2 cloves garlic, minced
- 1 teaspoon fresh ginger, grated
- Red pepper flakes (optional, for heat)

For the Pork and Cabbage:

- 1.5 to 2 pounds pork tenderloin or pork loin, trimmed
- 1 small head of green cabbage, thinly sliced
- 2 tablespoons vegetable oil
- Salt and black pepper, to taste
- Sesame seeds and sliced green onions (for garnish, optional)

Instructions:

Preheat the Oven:

   Preheat your oven to 400°F (200°C).
   Prepare Hoisin Glaze:
   - In a small bowl, whisk together hoisin sauce, soy sauce, honey, rice vinegar, sesame oil, minced garlic, grated ginger, and red pepper flakes (if using). Set aside.

   Prepare Pork and Cabbage:
   - Place the pork tenderloin or pork loin in the center of a large baking sheet.
   - Arrange the thinly sliced cabbage around the pork.

   Brush with Hoisin Glaze:
   - Brush the pork with the hoisin glaze, ensuring it's well coated.

- Drizzle the remaining hoisin glaze over the sliced cabbage.

Season with Salt and Pepper:
- Drizzle the vegetable oil over the cabbage.
- Season both the pork and cabbage with salt and black pepper to taste.

Roast in the Oven:
- Roast in the preheated oven for about 25-30 minutes or until the pork reaches an internal temperature of 145°F (63°C) and the cabbage is tender, stirring the cabbage halfway through.

Broil (Optional):
- If you want a caramelized finish on the pork, you can broil for an additional 2-3 minutes, keeping a close eye to prevent burning.

Rest and Slice:
- Allow the pork to rest for a few minutes before slicing it into medallions.

Garnish and Serve:
- Garnish the Hoisin Glazed Sheet Pan Pork with Cabbage with sesame seeds and sliced green onions if desired.

Serve:
- Serve the pork slices over the hoisin-glazed cabbage.

Enjoy your Hoisin Glazed Sheet Pan Pork with Cabbage, a flavorful and well-balanced meal that's perfect for a weeknight dinner!

Lemon Garlic Butter Baked Cod with Roasted Vegetables

Ingredients:

For the Lemon Garlic Butter Sauce:

- 1/4 cup unsalted butter, melted
- 3 cloves garlic, minced
- Zest of 1 lemon
- Juice of 1 lemon
- 2 tablespoons chopped fresh parsley
- Salt and black pepper, to taste

For the Cod and Vegetables:

- 4 cod fillets
- 1 pound baby potatoes, halved
- 1 bunch asparagus, trimmed
- 1 cup cherry tomatoes, halved
- 2 tablespoons olive oil
- Salt and black pepper, to taste

Instructions:

Preheat the Oven:

> Preheat your oven to 400°F (200°C).
> Prepare Lemon Garlic Butter Sauce:
> - In a small bowl, combine melted butter, minced garlic, lemon zest, lemon juice, chopped fresh parsley, salt, and black pepper. Set aside.
>
> Prepare Cod and Vegetables:
> - Pat the cod fillets dry with paper towels.
> - In a large mixing bowl, toss the halved baby potatoes, trimmed asparagus, and cherry tomatoes with olive oil, salt, and black pepper.
>
> Assemble on Baking Sheet:
> - Place the cod fillets on a baking sheet lined with parchment paper.
> - Arrange the seasoned vegetables around the cod.

Brush with Lemon Garlic Butter:
- Brush the cod fillets and vegetables with the prepared lemon garlic butter sauce, ensuring they are well coated.

Roast in the Oven:
- Roast in the preheated oven for about 15-20 minutes or until the cod is cooked through and flakes easily with a fork, and the vegetables are tender.

Broil (Optional):
- If you desire a golden finish, you can broil for an additional 2-3 minutes, keeping a close eye to prevent burning.

Check Doneness:
- Ensure the internal temperature of the cod reaches 145°F (63°C).

Garnish and Serve:
- Garnish the Lemon Garlic Butter Baked Cod with Roasted Vegetables with additional chopped fresh parsley.
- Serve hot.

Enjoy your Lemon Garlic Butter Baked Cod with Roasted Vegetables, a light and delightful meal that's perfect for a healthy and satisfying dinner!

Honey Mustard Glazed Chicken with Brussels Sprouts

Ingredients:

For the Honey Mustard Glaze:

- 1/4 cup Dijon mustard
- 3 tablespoons honey
- 2 tablespoons whole-grain mustard
- 2 tablespoons olive oil
- 2 cloves garlic, minced
- 1 teaspoon dried thyme
- Salt and black pepper, to taste

For the Chicken and Brussels Sprouts:

- 4 bone-in, skin-on chicken thighs
- 1 pound Brussels sprouts, trimmed and halved
- 2 tablespoons olive oil
- Salt and black pepper, to taste
- Lemon wedges (for serving, optional)
- Fresh parsley, chopped (for garnish, optional)

Instructions:

Preheat the Oven:

    Preheat your oven to 400°F (200°C).
    Prepare Honey Mustard Glaze:
- In a small bowl, whisk together Dijon mustard, honey, whole-grain mustard, olive oil, minced garlic, dried thyme, salt, and black pepper. Set aside.

    Prepare Chicken and Brussels Sprouts:
- Pat the chicken thighs dry with paper towels.
- In a large mixing bowl, toss the chicken thighs and halved Brussels sprouts with olive oil, salt, and black pepper until well coated.

    Assemble on Baking Sheet:
- Place the chicken thighs on a baking sheet lined with parchment paper, skin side up.
- Arrange the seasoned Brussels sprouts around the chicken.

    Brush with Honey Mustard Glaze:

- Brush the chicken thighs with the honey mustard glaze, reserving some for later.
- Toss the Brussels sprouts with a portion of the glaze.

Roast in the Oven:
- Roast in the preheated oven for about 30-35 minutes or until the chicken is cooked through and the skin is golden and crispy, turning the chicken and stirring the Brussels sprouts halfway through.

Check Doneness:
- Ensure the internal temperature of the chicken reaches 165°F (74°C).

Drizzle with Remaining Glaze:
- Drizzle the remaining honey mustard glaze over the chicken and Brussels sprouts.

Garnish and Serve:
- Garnish the Honey Mustard Glazed Chicken with Brussels Sprouts with chopped fresh parsley.
- Serve hot with lemon wedges on the side if desired.

Enjoy your Honey Mustard Glazed Chicken with Brussels Sprouts, a flavorful and comforting meal that's perfect for a family dinner or a special occasion!

Teriyaki Tempeh with Mixed Vegetables for a vegetarian option

Ingredients:

For the Teriyaki Marinade and Sauce:

- 1/3 cup soy sauce
- 3 tablespoons water
- 2 tablespoons rice vinegar
- 2 tablespoons mirin (sweet rice wine)
- 2 tablespoons brown sugar or maple syrup
- 1 tablespoon sesame oil
- 2 cloves garlic, minced
- 1 teaspoon fresh ginger, grated
- 1 tablespoon cornstarch (optional, for thickening)

For the Teriyaki Tempeh and Vegetables:

- 8 ounces tempeh, cut into cubes or slices
- 2 tablespoons vegetable oil
- 1 bell pepper, sliced
- 1 zucchini, sliced
- 1 carrot, julienned
- 1 cup broccoli florets
- 1 cup snap peas, trimmed
- Cooked brown or white rice (for serving)
- Sesame seeds and green onions (for garnish, optional)

Instructions:

Prepare Teriyaki Marinade and Sauce:
- In a small bowl, whisk together soy sauce, water, rice vinegar, mirin, brown sugar or maple syrup, sesame oil, minced garlic, and grated ginger. Set aside.
- If you want a thicker sauce, dissolve cornstarch in a tablespoon of water and whisk it into the sauce.

Marinate Tempeh:

- Place the tempeh cubes or slices in a shallow dish and pour half of the teriyaki sauce over them. Allow the tempeh to marinate for at least 15 minutes.

Cook Tempeh:
- In a large skillet or wok, heat vegetable oil over medium-high heat.
- Add the marinated tempeh and cook until browned on all sides, about 5-7 minutes.

Add Vegetables:
- Add bell pepper, zucchini, carrot, broccoli, and snap peas to the skillet. Stir-fry for an additional 5-7 minutes or until the vegetables are tender-crisp.

Pour Remaining Sauce:
- Pour the remaining teriyaki sauce over the tempeh and vegetables. Stir to coat everything evenly.

Serve:
- Serve the Teriyaki Tempeh with Mixed Vegetables over cooked brown or white rice.
- Garnish with sesame seeds and sliced green onions if desired.

Enjoy your Teriyaki Tempeh with Mixed Vegetables, a flavorful and wholesome vegetarian option that's perfect for a satisfying meal!

Sheet Pan Italian Sausage and Peppers

Ingredients:

- 1.5 pounds Italian sausage links (sweet or spicy, as per your preference)
- 3 bell peppers (red, green, and yellow), thinly sliced
- 1 large red onion, thinly sliced
- 3 tablespoons olive oil
- 2 teaspoons dried oregano
- 2 teaspoons dried basil
- 1 teaspoon garlic powder
- Salt and black pepper, to taste
- Crushed red pepper flakes (optional, for heat)
- Fresh parsley, chopped (for garnish, optional)

Instructions:

Preheat the Oven:

Preheat your oven to 400°F (200°C).
Prepare the Sausage and Vegetables:
- Place the Italian sausage links on a large baking sheet.
- Surround the sausages with the sliced bell peppers and red onions.

Drizzle with Olive Oil:
- Drizzle the olive oil over the sausages and vegetables.

Season with Herbs and Spices:
- Sprinkle dried oregano, dried basil, garlic powder, salt, black pepper, and crushed red pepper flakes (if using) evenly over the sausages and vegetables.

Toss to Coat:
- Toss everything together on the baking sheet, ensuring that the sausages and vegetables are coated with the olive oil and seasonings.

Arrange in a Single Layer:
- Arrange the sausages and vegetables in a single layer on the baking sheet for even cooking.

Roast in the Oven:

- Roast in the preheated oven for about 25-30 minutes or until the sausages are cooked through and the vegetables are tender and slightly caramelized.

Check Doneness:
- Ensure the internal temperature of the sausages reaches at least 160°F (71°C).

Garnish and Serve:
- Garnish the Sheet Pan Italian Sausage and Peppers with chopped fresh parsley if desired.

Serve:
- Serve the sausages and peppers hot, either on their own, in a sub roll, or over pasta.

Enjoy your Sheet Pan Italian Sausage and Peppers, a flavorful and hearty dish that's perfect for a quick and satisfying meal!

Baked Lemon Butter Shrimp with Zucchini and Cherry Tomatoes

Ingredients:

- 1 pound large shrimp, peeled and deveined
- 2 medium zucchini, sliced into half-moons
- 1 pint cherry tomatoes, halved
- 4 tablespoons unsalted butter, melted
- 3 tablespoons olive oil
- 3 cloves garlic, minced
- Zest of 1 lemon
- Juice of 1 lemon
- 1 teaspoon dried oregano
- Salt and black pepper, to taste
- Red pepper flakes (optional, for heat)
- Fresh parsley, chopped (for garnish)

Instructions:

Preheat the Oven:

Preheat your oven to 400°F (200°C).

Prepare Lemon Butter Mixture:
- In a small bowl, whisk together melted butter, olive oil, minced garlic, lemon zest, lemon juice, dried oregano, salt, black pepper, and red pepper flakes (if using).

Prepare Shrimp and Vegetables:
- Place the shrimp, sliced zucchini, and halved cherry tomatoes in a large mixing bowl.

Coat with Lemon Butter Mixture:
- Pour the lemon butter mixture over the shrimp and vegetables.
- Toss everything together until well coated.

Assemble in Baking Dish:
- Transfer the shrimp, zucchini, and cherry tomatoes to a baking dish, spreading them out in an even layer.

Bake in the Oven:

- Bake in the preheated oven for about 15-20 minutes or until the shrimp are pink and opaque, and the vegetables are tender, stirring halfway through for even cooking.

Broil (Optional):
- If you want a slightly charred finish, you can broil for an additional 2-3 minutes, keeping a close eye to prevent burning.

Check Doneness:
- Ensure the shrimp are fully cooked, and the internal temperature reaches 145°F (63°C).

Garnish and Serve:
- Garnish the Baked Lemon Butter Shrimp with Zucchini and Cherry Tomatoes with chopped fresh parsley.

Serve:
- Serve the dish hot, over rice, pasta, or with crusty bread for soaking up the delicious lemon butter sauce.

Enjoy your Baked Lemon Butter Shrimp with Zucchini and Cherry Tomatoes, a quick and flavorful dish perfect for a light and satisfying dinner!

www.ingramcontent.com/pod-product-compliance
Lightning Source LLC
LaVergne TN
LVHW081600060526
838201LV00054B/1984